Jeet Kune Do
From A to Z
(Volume Two)

Jeet Kune Do

From A to Z

VOLUME TWO

Chris Kent

UP **UNIQUE PUBLICATIONS**
Burbank, California

DISCLAIMER

Please note that the author and publisher of this book are NOT RESPONSI-BLE in any manner whatsoever for any injury that may result from practicing the techniques and/or following the instructions given within. Since the physical activities described herein may be too strenuous in nature for some readers to engage in safely, it is essential that a physician be consulted prior to training.

First published in 2000 by Unique Publications.

Library of Congress Catalog Number:
ISBN: 0-86568-178-3

Unique Publications
4201 Vanowen Place
Burbank, CA 91505
(800) 332–3330

First edition
05 04 03 02 01 00 99 98 97 1 3 5 7 9 10 8 6 4 2

Printed in the United States of America

Edited by Mark V. Wiley
Designed by Patrick Gross

DEDICATION

I would like to dedicate these books and tapes first and foremost to Leslie and Sarah Leilani, the two shining stars in my life.

Secondly, to all of my students and training partners who have aided in my own personal development.

ACKNOWLEDGEMENTS

I would like to thank my instructors for assisting me in the making of both the videotapes and these books:

Gordon Fong
John Turman
Randy Gaetano
Keith Jung
David Cheng
Jeff Scharlin
George Toy
Kevin Donovan
David Maldonado
David Renan

Also, thanks to John Soet, Curtis Wong, Jamie Itagaki, Jose Fraguas, Patrick Gross, and John Little without whom these books and tapes would not have been possible.

Contents

INTRODUCTION

Welcome to Volume Two of *Jeet Kune Do from A to Z.* In Volume One we concentrated on building a firm JKD foundation, and covered preliminary training elements including on-guard positioning, footwork and mobility, the various tools in the JKD weapons arsenal, and a complete breakdown of each of the five ways of attack.

In this volume we examine the more tactical elements required to become a complete fighter. In Chapter One we conclude our exploration in the art of the successful attack by examining the use of feints and false Attacks. In Chapter Two we explore the art and science of counter-attacking, including the use of interception, parry-and-counter, evade-and-counter, and jam-and-counter. Chapter Three offers you a breakdown of the various defensive skills used in JKD, and Chapters Four through Six are designed to increase your understanding of various tactical elements such as timing, distance, rhythm, cadence, and tempo. Some of the major philosophical tenets of Jeet Kune Do are explained in the Appendix section of the book.

As with the first volume, many of the principles and training methods illustrated in one chapter can and should be cross-referenced with those illustrated in another. All of the elements are interrelated. As I said in the introduction of Volume One, while these books do show certain techniques, techniques are not what they are about. The techniques are examples to illustrate the principles underlying the art. Use these two volumes along with the Training Journal (Volume Three) to help increase your understanding and working knowledge of Bruce Lee's art, science, and philosophy of unarmed combat. Remember: it's not how much you absorb, but how much of what you've absorbed that you can apply "alively." Read on!

Chapter 1

FEINTS, FALSE ATTACKS, AND COUNTER-TIME

"While direct attack is certainly used in JKD, most offensive action is indirect, meaning that it follows a feint or false attack, or takes the form of countering after an opponent's attack has been foiled."

—*Bruce Lee*

Would you simply charge in blindly against an opponent whom you have never met before, and of whom you have very little or no knowledge about? Or, like a lion as it enters an arena to face an adversary it has never seen, would you move cautiously before engaging such an opponent?

An intelligent fighter will keep himself out of an opponent's striking distance at first, cautiously feeling out his adversary and, if necessary, engaging him in a battle of wits. His primary objective at this point of the game should be to try to find out what type of offensive actions the opponent will use and also how he will react to actions made against him. Will he retreat, attempt to block or parry, or counter-attack? And one of the best methods to gather this information is through the use of feints and false attacks.

In Jeet Kune Do, the use of feints and false attacks is an integral part of both attack and counter-attack. The more you can catch an opponent off-guard or off-balance through the use of feints and false attacks, the greater your chances of success against him will be.

Feints

A feint is an offensive action that leads an opponent to believe that either a specific or a general attack is being launched against him. Its objective is to divert the opponent's attention from your final, or real point of attack. The idea behind feinting is to "send the opponent's thoughts somewhere else" for a split-second during the initial phase of your attack. Feints are used to make an opponent react, either with a defensive or counter-offensive action, allowing you to act on that reaction and execute the final, real attack. The four primary objectives of feinting are:

1) To make an opponent hesitate momentarily as you close the distance against him.

Photo Series 1-5: In this example, you feint a side kick to the opponent's midsection to make him hesitate as you close the distance, and then score with a spinning back kick.

2) To open the line in which you really intend to attack.

Photo Series 6–9: In this example, you use a low lead hook kick feint to draw the opponent's lead arm down in an attempt to block, then shift your attack and score with a lead hook kick to the head.

3) To deceive the opponent with one limb while striking him with another.

Photo Series 10–12: In this example you use a low lead front kick feint to draw the opponent's lead hand down to block, then shift your attack and score with a lead straight punch to the face.

4) To determine how the opponent reacts, so that you can deal with him.

Photo Series 13–15: In this example you use a low body drop feint to draw both of the opponent's arms down, then shift your attack and score with a lead hook kick to the head.

5) Feints can be divided into various categories, including:

Direction of Attack—This involves a feint of a change in your direction, such as moving to your right, appearing to switch to your left, and then suddenly attacking from the right.

Moving Forward or Backward—This involves using a forward or backward step to draw the opponent's action in order to counter it.

Angle of Attack—This involves switching your attack, such as feinting a lead straight punch then turning it into a lead uppercut midway through its motion.

Change of Weapon—This involves switching from one arm to the other, or one leg to the other, or from leg to arm or arm to leg.

Change of Levels—This involves switching the level of your actions, such as from the body to the head, from the head to the leg, etc.

Feints or false attacks can be made along any line. They can be used against the opponent's outside or inside lines, his low line or high line. By deliberately feinting into a certain line, it's possible for you to induce an opponent to gradually raise or lower his arms, attempt to adjust his distance with footwork, or change his on-guard position. For example, a number of feints in the opponent's high line could be used to pave the way for a sudden attack to the middle or low line, or vice versa.

Series 16–18: You can use a high lead hand feint to draw the opponent's attention upward in order to score with a low lead hook kick to his lead knee.

Photo Series 19–21: You can use a low lead hand feint to draw the opponent's lead arm down in order to score with a straight punch to his face.

Series 22–23: You can use a quick advance against the opponent to give the impression that you are punching, thus causing him to re-adjust his distance by retreating.

Simple and Compound Feints

Feints can be divided into two categories: simple and compound. A simple feint is comprised of a single motion, such as extending your arm, lifting your knee, or suddenly lowering your body.

Photo Series 24–25: Simple feint. You can use a lead leg knee lift to feint a low kick in order to draw the opponent's rear arm downward.

Photo Series 26–27: Simple feint. You can use a body drop feint to draw both of the opponent's arms downward.

A compound feint, on the other hand, is comprised of two or more motions used in conjunction, such as a low-kick feint followed by a high hand feint. Compound feints can be used in three basic ways: 1) vertically, such as from the low line to the high line; 2) laterally, such as from the outside line to the inside line; or 3) a combination of vertical and lateral, such as from the low inside line to the high outside line.

Photo Series 28–30: Vertical compound feint. Use a low straight-high-straight compound feint with your lead hand.

Photo Series 31–33: Vertical compound feint. Use a high lead-straight punch feint followed immediately by a low rear-straight punch feint.

Photo Series 34–36: Lateral compound feint. Feint a high lead straight punch followed immediately by a high lead hook feint.

Photo Series 37–39: Combination compound feint. Feint a low lead straight kick, followed by a high lead palm hook (lateral).

Types of Feints

Feints should be utilized at the low, middle, and high levels, and can be made using a single limb (such as an arm or leg), the body, footwork, or any combination thereof. The type of feint you choose to use can depend upon the type of reaction you seek to draw, as well as on the distance you are from the opponent. Some of the various methods of feinting that you can use include:

Arm Feints. The arm can be used to feint an upward or downward attack. It can be drawn back as if preparing to hit, or can feint a curved blow such as a hook or a backfist.

Photo Series 40–41: Arm feint. Use a lead shovel hook feint to the opponent's midsection to draw a reaction.

Leg Feints. The leg can be used to feint a kick by simply lifting the knee suddenly, or by using a small half-motion kick. Even a small, quick turn of the foot can be used.

Photo Series 42–43: Knee lift feint. Use a lead leg knee lift feint to give the opponent the impression that you are launching a low kick as you bridge the distance.

Photo Series 44–45: Half-kick Feint. Use a half motion kick feint to give the opponent the idea that you are attempting to kick low and draw his hands down.

Photo Series 46–47: Foot-turn Feint. By pivoting your lead foot and turning your body slightly, you can give the opponent the impression that you are throwing a lead hook to his head.

Body Feints. For body feints, you can use the action of the body to create the impression that an attack is being launched. Body feints include such things as the knee-bend feint, the body-drop feint, and the side-bend feint.

Photo Series 48–49: Knee-bend Feint—While advancing slowly, quickly bend the lead knee, giving the impression that the arms are moving as well as the body.

Photo Series 50–51: Body-drop Feint—Make a quick forward bend of the upper body, at the same time bending the lead knee and moving the lead hand slightly forward.

Photo Series 52–53: Side-bend Feint—Drop the body slightly forward and to the left, creating the impression that the lead hand is about to fire an attack.

Footwork Feints. You can use various types of footwork, such as a quick step forward or backward, or sidestepping to the right or left.

Photo Series 54–55: Step Forward Feint. Use a step forward combined with a lead arm swing to give the impression you are launching an attack

Photo Series 56–57: Sidestep Feint. Use a left sidestep to give the opponent the idea that you are going to attack from a different position.

Photo Series 58–59: Retreat-step Feint. Use a quick retreat step to give the opponent the idea that you are withdrawing to lure him into moving forward.

The following are examples of how to utilize various types of feints combined with follow-up actions:

Photo Series 60–62: Against an opponent in an unmatched lead, use a high lead hand feint to draw the opponent's lead arm up, then score with a low rear straight punch to the ribs.

Photo Series 63–65: Use a high lead-hand finger jab feint to the opponent's eyes to draw both of his hands up, then score with a low rear oblique kick to the shin.

Photo Series 66–68: Against an opponent in an unmatched lead, use a low body drop feint to draw the opponent's arms downward, then score with an inverted hook kick to the opponent's face.

Photo Series 69–71: Use a high lead hand feint to draw the opponent's lead arm up, then score with a low lead straight punch to the midsection

Photo Series 72–74: Feint a lead shovel hook to the opponent's solar plexus to draw his rear arm down, shift and score with a straight rear punch to the face.

Photo Series 75–77: Against an opponent in an unmatched lead, feint a low rear-straight punch to draw the opponent's lead arm down, score with a lead hook to the jaw.

Photo Series 78–80: Against an opponent in an unmatched lead, feint a low inverted hook kick with the lead leg to the groin to draw his lead arm down, score with a lead finger jab to the eyes.

Rhythm in Feinting

Any feint must be linked together with the real attacking motion. If your action is executed in distinct, separate movements, it will never deceive any parry because your opponent will find your arm or leg with his own before the conclusion of your action.

The rhythm when you use a simple feint with an attack should be *"long-short."* The word "long" as it's used in the context of feinting doesn't mean "slow." It means that your feint must penetrate deeply toward the opponent and force the opponent to react. It's a combination of speed and penetration. The word "short" means that the second part of the movement, the real attack, must be fast and decisive. The feint rhythm or cadence when using a compound feint with an attack is *"long-short-short."*

Finally, by knowing the speed of an opponent, you can change your own speed and "break the rhythm" of your feints. For example, if you use a two-motion feint followed by a real attack, and you set the cadence or rhythm as "long-short-short," you can suddenly change it to "short-long-short" in order to mislead the opponent and make him believe that the second feint is actually your real attack.

Speed of Feinting

The speed of any type of feint you use is crucial. It has to be regulated to the opponent's reaction speed if it is to be successful. If you shift your feint too quickly, before the opponent has reacted to your feint, your real attack may end up in a still-closed line. Whereas if you hold your feint too long, the opponent may have time to counter-hit you before you have a chance to complete your real attack. So you should attempt to discover, as quickly as possible, the cadence or speed of the opponent.

Photo Series 81–82: Shifting the feint too quickly. By shifting from a low body feint to a high lead hook kick before the opponent has reacted to the feint, your kick may land on a still-covered line.

Photo Series 83–84: Holding the feint too long. By holding the body-drop feint too long before shifting into your final attack, you may be hit by the opponent in the midst of your actions.

False Attacks

A false attack differs from a feint in that it is an attack that is purposely designed to fall short of its target, yet travels deep enough to either draw a reaction or ascertain the opponent's reactions. It is not a real attack, but a calculated feint made in order to elude the opponent's defensive action. A false attack must be made with such decision that the opponent will react just as if it were a real attack.

Photo Series 85–86: In this example of using a false attack, you fire a high lead straight punch that is purposely designed to fall short of hitting the opponent.

Photo Series 87–88: In this example, you use a low lead straight punch.

One of the primary uses of false attacks is as a set-up for other forms of attack such as the Progressive Indirect Attack (PIA) or the Attack By Combination (ABC).

False Attack with PIA

Photo Series 89–92: In this example, you use a low lead hook kick false attack to close the distance, followed by a high lead straight punch false attack to draw the opponent's inward block, which you deceive and score with a straight rear cross.

False Attack with ABC

Photo Series 93–94: In this example, you use a lead straight punch to ascertain how the opponent reacts. In this case he attempts to use an inward block.

Photo Series 95–97: Having ascertained the opponent's defensive reaction, you use the lead straight punch false attack to draw the opponent's inward block, then deceive the block and score with a straight rear punch to the face.

Rhythm in False Attacks

As with feints, by changing the cadence or speed of your action, you can break the rhythm and mislead the opponent or disrupt his sense of timing.

Photo Series 98–102: Using the same example as shown previously, use the lead leg and lead hand false attack sequence, but insert a split-second pause to disrupt the opponent's timing as he attempts to parry, then score with the rear cross.

Speed in False Attacks

As with feints, the speed of your false attack has to be regulated to fit in with the opponent. If it is too fast, the opponent may not react to it, and if it's too slow, the opponent might counter-hit you in the midst of your actions.

Training Tips for Feints and False Attacks

- A good feint should appear so real that an opponent has no choice but to react. It should be decisive, expressive, and above all, threatening. As Bruce Lee stated, "Your feint should make the opponent feel faint." At the same time, however, your feint must seem to be a simple attacking movement. If the opponent can sense it's a trap, he won't go for it.

- Every feint or false attack involves the risk of a momentary exposure to a stop-hit or time-hit. Therefore, make all of your movements as small as possible, with the least deviation necessary to make the opponent react.

- Good timing is essential for the most effective use of feints. Your feint must surprise the opponent when his sense of judgment and his possibilities of movement are more limited. Ferret out your opponent's actions with forays so well-timed as to prevent the opponent from attacking during the foray itself.

- Remember, the more feints you use in any offensive action, the greater the chances that the opponent can either counter-attack or escape out of range. Therefore, never use more feints than necessary to get the job done.

- Whenever you execute a feint or false attack, you need to be ready to deal with each and all of the opponent's potential reactions. Always maintain a well-covered position and be in balance to parry a stop-hit or time-hit that might be attempted by the opponent.

- Not all attempts at feinting will go smoothly. The unpredicted response must always be allowed for. Therefore, always have a second line of defense.

You can increase your chances of success by combining your feints and false attacks with:

- Simple Attacks from Immobility. Use a series of feints or false attacks to "motor-set" the opponent to expect a preparation or a complex action, then surprise him with a swift and unannounced simple movement.

- Variation of Rhythm or Cadence. Use a series of carefully slowed-down feints and slow forward and backward footwork actions to "put the opponent to sleep," then suddenly erupt with a simple movement at highest speed to catch him unaware.

Dealing with Feints and False Attacks

The primary factor in dealing with feints and false attacks is to learn to recognize a true threat versus a feint or false attack. This requires awareness. You must do your best to distinguish between an opponent's false attacks and his real attacks, and try to ignore all his testing forays. Never believe in any of your opponent's threats or feints. Keep in mind that they usually conceal a trap. Keep cool while awaiting the opponent's attack and take great care not to show in advance what you will parry when actually attacked. Acquire an air of unpredictability so that you can keep the opponent guessing.

Conclusion

The purpose of a feint or false attack is to mislead the opponent, to bring him into motion, and to create and ensure the most favorable distance for the final attack. The action of the feint is to make the arm or leg elude the opponent's parries or defensive action before the conclusion of the attack. The variety of feints has practically no limit. Feints can be slow or fast, long or short, simple or compound, depending on the opponent's reactions. You should know in advance the openings that will be created by each particular feint. A good martial artist knows what openings will result before he feints, and makes use of this knowledge and initiates his follow-up action almost before the opening results. Finally, feints used too often will defeat their very purpose. So use them judiciously and combine them with real, economical, simple attacks so that the opponent won't know whether a simple attack or a feint followed by a deception is being used.

Counter-Time in Attack

Counter-time is the action of using some form of invitation to draw a stop-hit from an opponent, then parrying or evading it, and countering from it. Counter-time is a highly effective strategy to use against an opponent whose combative game is built on counter-offensive actions, and who either has a predilection for stop-hitting, or who continually attacks into your attack.

Where counter-time differs from counter-attack is that counter-time is intentionally set up by you as the attacker. Counter-time depends on drawing an opponent's stop-hit so that it can be parried and countered. It requires cool anticipation of the opponent's counter-attack, and excellent timing. The invitation used to draw the opponent's counter-attack has to be made convincingly. It must induce the opponent to attempt to stop-hit you, but not be so obvious as to warn him of the intended sequel. Success in using counter-time depends on concealing your real intentions and inducing the opponent to make his stop-hit land with conviction, so that he has little or no opportunity to recover when it's parried before your own attack lands.

Counter-time can be used with various preparations such as:

- Intentionally uncovered feints.

- Sudden advances against the opponent.

- Attacks against the opponent's arms.

Photo Series 103–105: Intentionally Uncovered Feint. You can use a low lead hand feint while keeping your guard open in order to draw the opponent's right rear cross, which you then counter with a rear sliding finger jab.

Photo Series 106–108: Sudden
Advance. You can use a sudden push
shuffle advance to move toward the
opponent and draw his attempted
stop-hit, which you then counter
with a simultaneous rear hand parry
and lead hand strike.

Photo Series 109–111: Attack Against Arm. You can use a lead hand "beat" against the inside of the opponent's lead arm to draw the opponent's rear cross, which you then counter with a simultaneous rear hand parry and lead hand strike.

Timing in Counter-Time

Proper tempo in using counter-time is crucial. By choosing the proper moment, you can eliminate in the opponent any notion of a possible trap and make the preparation so real that the opponent's counter-attack is almost instinctive.

Chapter 2

THE ART OF COUNTER-ATTACKING

"It is the greatest art in fighting, the art of the champion."
—*Bruce Lee*

There's a basic theory in combat that states, "For every attack there is a counter." It's a simple fact that any offensive movement made by an opponent will expose some part of his body. It doesn't matter how good an opponent is, when he attacks you, he's going to offer you either an opening somewhere, or at least the opportunity to interrupt his attack before its completion.

A counter-attack is an attack made against an opponent's offensive movement, either as he attacks on his own initiative or is somehow provoked into attacking.

The objective when using any form of counter-attack is to avoid being hit while at the same time succeed in hitting the opponent while he is still out of position or is off-balance as a result of missing you with his attack. Don't look at counter-attack as a defensive action, but rather as an attacking action, an advanced form of offense in which you use the opponent's offensive action as a means to successfully complete your own attack. In counter-attack, you "move second but arrive first."

To achieve the highest levels of success when using a counter-attack, you need to shift your attitude into an "attack-oriented" mode, and learn to think "hit" instead of "block." For example, if your opponent launches a rear cross toward your face and all you can think of is that he is six-foot-five, weighs 250 pounds and is about to smash your face . . . he will smash your face. Instead, you've got to think to yourself, "Wow! What a great opportunity this opponent is giving me to side kick him in his knee," etc. Instead of thinking that your opponent is going to hurt you, concern yourself instead with the havoc you're going to wreak upon him after he's been so kind as to put himself in the position where you can reach him.

In Jeet Kune Do, counter-attacking involves all methods of hitting, kicking, trapping, and grappling, as well as all of the main techniques of evasion such as parrying, slipping, bobbing and weaving, ducking, sidestepping, feinting, and so on. There are two types of counter-attacks: offensive and defensive-offensive. Offensive counter-attacks include the stop-hit or stop-kick. Defensive-offensive counter-attacks include the time-hit as well as the use of parry-and-counter, evade-and-counter, and jam-and-counter methods. Below we examine the various forms of counter-attack used in Jeet Kune Do.

The Stop-Hit

In an episode of the 1970s television series "Longstreet" aptly titled *The Way of the Intercepting Fist,"* the character Bruce Lee portrays is asked by another character to explain the martial art that he does. Lee tells the man, "Try to touch me, anyway you can . . ." The moment the man moves toward him, Lee intercepts him with a lightning fast side-kick to the lead knee, then tells him, "To reach me, you must move to me. Your movement offers me an opportunity to intercept you . . ."

Jeet Kune Do is about interception. In fact, the name of the art says it all: *"The Way of the Intercepting Fist."* JKD eschews the normal block-and-then-hit response that is favored by many martial art systems. Rather than blocking an opponent's attack, in JKD you seek to intercept it with your own attack in such a way as to nullify or destroy it. In this way, defense becomes almost a side effect of offense. Your attack or counter-attack literally becomes your defense. Why should you waste your strength and energy and run the risk of getting hit in an attempt to block a blow when you can stop-hit the opponent instead? After all, isn't it more economical and efficient to accomplish the same results by using one motion as opposed to two?

Many people tend to confuse stop-hitting an opponent with the act of simply sticking out an arm or leg and allowing the opponent to run into it when they attack. However, this is not the case. A stop-hit is an aggressive offensive motion that arrests or "stops" the opponent in the development of his attack. Stop-hits are designed to score in the midst of the attacker's action and must land before his action is completed. To be successful, a stop-hit must be performed swiftly, unexpectedly, and with the greatest possible power and determination.

Decision, preparation, and resolve are all key elements when using any type of stop-hit. Used properly, they can have a devastating effect on an opponent's morale. Every time he attempts to launch an attack or makes a preparation to attack, he is hit and "stopped in his tracks."

Timing the Stop-Hit

When using a stop-hit, timing and speed are of the essence. A fraction of a second can mean the difference between success and failure. To stop-hit effectively you need excellent judgment, precise timing, and correct distance. There are several moments in the course of fighting when an opportunity to stop-hit an opponent may present itself:

You can intercept on the opponent's preparation. A preparation includes anything an opponent does before actually initiating his attack, such as taking a step forward, or winding up before throwing a punch.

Photo Series 1–2: You can use a lead straight punch to the face to intercept the opponent as he takes a step forward in preparation to attack

Photo Series 3–4: You can use a lead-leg side-kick to the opponent's lead leg as he takes a step forward in preparation to attack.

You can intercept the opponent in the midst of his attacking motion. In this case the attack has already been launched and is on its way.

Photo Series 5–6: You can use a lead straight punch to the face to stop-hit the opponent as he is in the midst of throwing a low rear cross.

Photo Series 7–9: You can use a lead-leg side kick to intercept the opponent as he is in the midst of throwing a lead straight punch. (Note the upper body lean away for added safety).

You can intercept an opponent between two motions of a compound movement.

Photo Series 10–12: You can use an upper body "snap-away" to avoid the opponent's lead straight punch, then stop-hit him with your lead hand as he is shifting into a lead hook attack.

You can intercept the opponent if he makes wide, swinging movements.

Photo Series 13–14: You can use a lead straight punch to stop-hit the opponent as he attacks with a wide, looping lead-hand hook.

You can also intercept an opponent when he is preoccupied with his own feints or plans of attack. The best moment to execute a stop-hit is at the very beginning of an opponent's attack, such as the split-second he moves the leading foot when beginning an advance, or at his very first feint. This surprises and tends to block his reflexive actions, preventing him from completing the attack or delaying the final movement of his action. He cannot suddenly reverse his movement and "change horses in midstream." The longer you wait when using a stop-hit, the greater the risk factor becomes. This is because the further an opponent's attack develops toward you, the more speed and power it will have behind it. If you wait until the opponent's attack is almost upon you, it will be very difficult to stop-hit.

Photo Series 15–16: By waiting too long before launching your stop-hit, the opponent's attack will have gained speed and power, making it very difficult to stop-hit effectively and safely.

Oftentimes, when using a stop-hit it's necessary to either take a step forward, or at least use a slight forward lean in order to land your attack ahead of the opponent.

Photo 17: At a longer distance you might combine a forward step with your stop-hit in order to "beat the opponent to the punch."

Photo 18: At a closer distance you might use a forward body lean with your stop-hit in order to land your attack ahead of the opponent.

You should be able to stop-hit or stop-kick an opponent the split-second an opening occurs. Train yourself to be constantly prepared to stop-hit or kick with speed and accuracy from any angle during the course of any movement.

Finally, a note of caution concerning the use of stop-hits. Some people tend to rely on the use of the stop-hit as their sole method of counter-attack. This is dangerous. If you try to use stop-hitting too often, you run the risk that a smart opponent may draw your stop-hit and counter it. So use the stop-hit judiciously and combine it with other forms of counter-attack.

The Time-Hit

The second method of counter-attacking is called a time-hit. In essence, a time-hit is a stop-hit that scores while at the same time preventing the opponent's attack from landing. The time-hit differs from a pure stop-hit insomuch as it anticipates and intercepts the final line of the attack, and is delivered in such a way that it closes the line while carrying the opponent's attacking limb away. The forward motion of your extending limb deflects the opponent's limb as you force your way toward the target, thereby protecting your own. In this way you are covered, either with in-line covering or with supplementary covering.

The time-hit is actually considered the safest form of counter-attack. Like the stop-hit, the time-hit requires a highly developed sense of timing, a keen eye, and control of your tools. And, like when using a stop-hit, conception and execution must take place instantaneously. A good moment (tempo) to counter is when an opponent is executing a movement because he cannot reverse the movement and "change horses in midstream."

Photo Series 19–20: Against an opponent in an unmatched lead, you can use a lead-hand sliding finger jab against the opponent's lead straight punch to simultaneously deflect his line of attack and score.

The successful use of any type of time-hit requires three things:

- Correct anticipation of the opponent's attacking intentions. You need to know or be able to anticipate what line the opponent's attack will come in.

- Precise placement of your counter-attack weapon in the path of the final movement of attack.

- Precision in hitting the available target.

Photo Series 21–22: You can use a rear-hand sliding finger jab against the opponent's rear straight punch to simultaneously close the line of attack and score.

Photo Series 23–24: Against an opponent who is in the same lead as you, you can use a lead-hand sliding leverage hit against his attempted rear uppercut to the body.

Sometimes when using a time-hit, it might be necessary to angle your body in order to dominate the opponent's attacking limb. Also, like the stop-hit, in order to increase the effectiveness of a time-hit, you should reinforce it with either a small advancing action or a slight forward lean.

Correct Timing

Like any other form of counter-attack, timing is crucial when using a time-hit. If you attempt to time-hit too early, an opponent can switch his line of attack, and if you wait too long the opponent's attack might score.

Photo Series 25–28: By attempting to use a time-hit too early against an opponent's lead straight punch, you may allow the opponent to switch his line of attack, in this case into a lead hook to the head.

Photo Series 29–30: By waiting too long before using a lead straight punch to time-hit the opponent's lead straight punch, you may allow the opponent's attack to score.

Training Tips

The following factors can increase your possibilities of success in using either a stop-hit or a time-hit:

- Maintain proper focus of attention. You have to concentrate fully on the opponent and not let yourself wander mentally. Keep your mind on the task at hand.

- Develop good neuromuscular coordination skills. It will do you little or no good if, when you see the opportunity to use a stop-hit or a time-hit, you cannot get your body to respond as quickly as necessary.

- Keep relaxed. Muscular tenseness tightens and thereby slows your movements down.

- Maintain your offensive determination. You've got to want to score against the opponent. A split-second hesitation on your part and the opportunity may be gone.

- Develop the ability to "read the opponent" and spot any signs of telegraphing on his part, such as withdrawing his arm before punching, etc.

Interception requires tools, awareness, and a level of intention or "emotional content" in any situation. To intercept an opponent's attack without intention is really nothing more than a mere block. It is defensive and will do little or nothing to slow your opponent's attack. He'll keep on coming. You may block a hundred of his strikes this way and you won't stop him, slow him down (except maybe by fatigue), or in any way diminish his intention or course of action. But if you intercept him with intention, with "emotional content," you break his attack and replace the energy of his intention with your own. He must now respond to your intention.

Parry and Counter

The third form of counter-attack is the "Parry and Counter." While parrying is a defensive action and will be covered in depth in the chapter on Defensive Skills, what we're going to look at in this section is the way parrying may be used with counter-attacking. There are three different timings that you can use when combining a parry with your counter-attack. The first is a parry-followed by counter, wherein you first parry the opponent's attack, then launch your counter-attack. Rhythmically, the action takes place on two separate and distinct beats.

Photo Series 31–33: Parry followed by counter. This example illustrates how you can use a high inside parry followed by a lead straight punch.

When using this method of counter-attack, your counter-action may be immediate or delayed. You could counter immediately following your

parry, or you might delay your counter a moment in order to observe how the opponent recovers after his attack has failed. This variation of cadence can be used to disconcert the opponent or may make him disclose his reactions to the riposte prematurely. A simple counter consists of a single action which may be either direct (straight) or indirect (disengage). A compound counter consists of two or more movements, one of which may be a feint.

Structurally speaking, while parry-and-then-counter may be the slowest of the three methods, this form of countering can be very useful if you suddenly find yourself caught unawares by an opponent, or if the opponent is much faster than you.

The second method is the "Simultaneous Parry and Counter." In this case your parry and the counter-attack take place at exactly the same time and on a single beat.

Photo Series 34–35: Simultaneous Parry and Counter. This example illustrates how you can parry and counter-hit the opponent at the same time.

The third method of countering is the "Counter followed by Parry." This is the fastest and most efficient method, in which you counter-hit the opponent first and then parry only as necessary.

Photo Series 36–38: Counter followed by Parry. In this case, you "beat the opponent to the punch" and hit him first, then parry afterwards.

When using either the "parry-and-then-counter" or the "simultaneous parry-and-counter," it's most effective if you apply your parry at the moment the opponent's attack is completing its course. At this point the time available to the opponent to change from attack to defense is cut to the minimum, and your counter will stand a much better chance of scoring before the opponent can either evade or parry it. Also, it is important to regulate your distance accordingly.

Jam and Counter

"Jamming" is another method that can be used to offset an opponent's attack and put you in a good position to counter-attack. When you jam an opponent's attack you crash into the attacking line in a well-covered position, nullifying it and putting you in a position to shift into close-range fighting ranges, such as trapping or grappling. It is important to jam the opponent's attack as early as possible, before the attack has had time to gain speed and power. You should also make sure that you are in a well-balanced position to prevent yourself from being knocked over by the opponent's attack.

Photo Series 39–41: Jamming an Attack. The moment the opponent starts to launch his lead leg kick, you can slide forward to jam it with your own leg and prevent it from being delivered, while simultaneously covering the opponent's lead arm to prevent it from being used. Immediately after jamming the kick, shift into grappling using a rear neck choke.

Evade and Counter

The final method of countering is "Evade and Counter." As with parrying, a complete breakdown of the various methods of evasion will be covered in the chapter on Defensive Skills. What we will look at here is how evasion can be used in counter-attacking. In evasion, you avoid an attack by using footwork or body movement and angulation to either open the distance and cause the attack to miss, or stay in range and shift under or away from it.

Photo Series 42–44: Against a lead side kick to your midsection, you can use a curving right step combined with a rear-hand semicircular parry, then counter with a lead straight punch to the face.

Photo Series 45–48: Against the same lead side kick to the midsection, you can use a lead-hand semicircular parry combined with a curving left step, then counter with a rear neck choke.

Photo Series 49–51: Against a high lead straight punch, you can use a curving right step to evade the blow without even parrying, then counter with your own lead straight punch.

Photo Series 52–54: Against the same lead straight punch, you can use a curving left step to evade the punch, then counter with rear shovel hook to the kidney.

When using any form of counter-attacking, three factors should be analyzed and understood. The first is that whatever type of offensive action the opponent uses will help determine which areas of his body are (or will be) vulnerable to attack. For example, a lead hand or foot attack will expose the lead side of the opponent's body, **(Photos 55–56)** whereas a rear hand or leg attack will expose his centerline and the entire front of his body **(Photos 57–58)**.

The second factor is whether the counter-attack should be one or two-handed. Blocking, guarding, and parrying leave one hand free to counter with, whereas sidestepping, slipping, ducking, and bobbing and weaving allow either hand to counter.

Photo Series 59–61: Against a lead straight punch, you can combine a left sidestep with your own lead straight counter, then follow-up with a straight rear cross to the face.

Photo Series 62–64: Against a high straight rear cross, you can use a right sidestep to evade the blow first, then counter with a lead shovel hook to the opponent's ribs.

Photo Series 65–67: You can use a lead-hand cross parry to an opponent's lead straight punch, while at the same time countering with a low rear straight punch to the opponent's midsection.

Photo Series 68–69: Against an opponent's high rear cross, you can slip to the outside position and simultaneously counter with a left rear cross to the face.

Photo Series 70–72: Against the same rear cross, you can also slip outside and then counter with a lead shovel hook to the opponent's ribs. In this case the slip is done first, then the counter-punch is thrown.

Photo Series 73–75: You can duck underneath the opponent's rear hook punch and counter with a rear straight punch to the opponent's groin.

Photo Series 76–78: You can duck under the opponent's rear hook punch and counter with your lead straight punch to the groin instead.

The third factor is that your counter-attack depends upon the method you use in avoiding the opponent's attack, as well as the type of attack itself.

Photo Series 79–80: You can avoid the opponent's lead straight punch by leaning away from it while at the same time countering with a low lead-leg side kick.

Photo Series 81–83: You can duck under an opponent's rear hook aimed at your head, and then shift into a grappling maneuver, such as a double leg attack.

Photo Series 84–85: You can evade an opponent's high rear hook kick by dropping your body low and using a low rear hook kick to attack the opponent's supporting leg.

The decision as to what kind of counter you choose to use depends partly on the way the opponent reacts when his attack has been parried. For example, does he attempt to retreat out of distance or continue forward with another form of attack? The speed of the opponent's recovery and the tactical intent are also determining factors in whether you counter from the ready position, or with an advance, etc. Does the opponent immediately recover back to his on-guard position or is he slow?

Defense Against Counter-Attacks

Basically, the best defense against counter-attacks is to give an opponent as little opportunity as possible to use them. Offensively, the best tactics are to (a) use mainly simple attacks and avoid offensive actions that are too complex or require too much movement, and (b) be prepared automatically to offset any counter the opponent might try to use. Defensively, the best tactic is to use second-intention in order to draw the opponent's counter, and then offset it with counter-time.

Training Tips

- Be aware of your position at all times in order direct your counter-attack to the target that is most vulnerable and where it will be most effective.

- Develop lightning-fast movements, the ability to adapt to and "fit-in" with the opponent, skillful deception, and the ability to anticipate the moment of the opponent's offensive actions.

- Don't hesitate with your counter. It should be a continuous motion (except when you use a delayed return).

- Every time an opponent tries to attack you, make them pay for it.

- Learn to stay cool and calm while awaiting an opponent's attack.

Conclusion

Counter-attacking skills are a vital part of your combative arsenal. Successful counter-attacking calls for great skill, perfect planning, and precise execution of technique. Besides a mastery of technique, you need precise timing, unerring judgment, and cool, calculating poise. Counter-attack calls for the closest power of observation and skill in defense. The depth, speed, firmness, and rhythm of the opponent's attack must be perceived. When you're training or sparring, study the opponent's delivery methods. Look for any signs of telegraphing and develop your ability to "read" your opponent's intentions and react before he does. Learn to intercept not only the opponent's thoughts, but also his actions. Finally, mix and vary your counter-attacks in order to reduce your predictability.

Chapter 3

THE ART OF DEFENSE

Most times, in Jeet Kune Do, defense is considered almost a side effect of constant attack, whereby you concentrate upon neutralizing an attacker as your own simultaneous attack is launched. However, while attack and counter-attack are given priority, good defensive skills are important and necessary. Intercepting an attack or counter-attacking may not be possible at a particular moment.

Perhaps your awareness or timing is off. Or maybe an opponent is faster or stronger and suddenly overwhelms you or tags you with a good shot. At times like these your defensive skills may well make the difference between victory and defeat. As Lee wrote in his personal notes, "Almost every fighter at one time or the other reaches a point where he loses some of his command, and must protect himself. When this time comes it is wise to have learned good defense."

This being the case, the learning of defensive skills is necessary and should include a wide variety of techniques. Defense is anything that opposes attack and either prevents it from scoring, or renders it less effective. There are four basic methods of defense. These are:

Footwork—control and regulation of distance.

Parries—actions of the hand that deflect an attack.

Evasion—body movements such as ducking, slipping, etc.

Blocking—placing something in the path of an attack.

Footwork

Strong footwork skills allow you to control and regulate the distance to get out of the way of an opponent's attack, thereby causing it to miss. The better your footwork, the more elusive you can be. And an elusive, moving target is harder to hit than a stationary one. The more adept you are at using footwork, the less you have to make use of your arms and legs in avoiding kicks and punches.

Used properly, footwork can actually become an aggressive deterrent when sparring. It can also be used as a means of reconnaissance to study the opponent.

There are two methods of using footwork in defense. The first is to open the distance, usually with some form of retreat. This type of defensive action will usually mean that you won't be in position to counter-attack without first re-closing the distance. The second is to move off-line from the attack and evade it by sidestepping (see the section on Footwork in Counter-Attack).

Photo Series 1–3: You can use a slide-step retreat to open the distance and evade an attack such as a side kick.

Photo Series 4–6: You can use a step-through retreat to open the distance and evade an attack such as a rear hook kick. When using this type of footwork you will finish in the opposite lead from the one you started in.

Photo Series 7–9: You can use a push shuffle retreat to open the distance and evade an opponent's punching attack, such as a lead hook.

Parrying

A parry is a defensive motion of the hand that is used to deflect an attack from its original path. As opposed to a block, which is force-against-force, a parry is a light, easy movement that relies on timing. The objective of a parry is to deflect the opponent's incoming energy rather than meeting it head-on. A parry might be a straight across motion, such as a rear-hand cross parry. Or it might be a curving, or semi-circular motion, such as a lead-hand hooking parry. The prime requirements of any parry is that it (a) provides sufficient protection, and (b) ensures conditions for immediate countering. In Jeet Kune Do, the major types of parries include:

    1. Lateral (right to left, left to right, while staying on a horizontal line)

    2. Semi-circular (travels in a semi-circular arc high to low or low to high)

    3. Circular (describes a circular motion)

Circular parries are generally used much less frequently than lateral and semi-circular parries due to the increased time factor involved.

When using a parry, the idea is not so much to knock the opponent's attacking limb aside, but to place a barrier into the line on which the attack is launched. In parrying, you should feel that in deflecting an opponent's punch or kick, you are literally "taking possession of it," and that through the contact you obtain with the attacking tool, you'll feel your opponent's reactions when he realizes that his attack has failed. The following points should be remembered when using any parry:

Never parry a blow until the last moment, just before it's about to hit you. The reason for this is that if you reach out when parrying, you will not only create openings for counter blows, but also give the opponent an opportunity to switch his attack onto another line.

Photo Series 10–12: This example illustrates how you wait until the opponent's blow is just about to reach you before you parry it with your rear-hand cross parry.

Photo Series 13–14: This example illustrates the danger of attempting to parry the opponent's blow too early, which allows him to shift his attack into another line and score with a lead hook to the head.

Control your motion. Your parry should stop as soon as the attack is deflected. If you over-parry or parry too hard, you can give an extra "push" to the opponent's tool which he may be able to use to his advantage by switching his attack onto another line, or launching a follow-up motion. You might also inadvertently knock his arm into your own counter-attack. Think of using your parry to "close the door" on an attack rather than "slamming the door." But make sure your parry is sufficient to deflect the blow. If you under-parry, the opponent's blow still may hit you.

Photo Series 15–16: This example illustrates how your lead-hand cross-parry should halt as soon as the opponent's attack has cleared your body.

Photo Series 17–18: This example illustrates the danger of over-parrying, which allows the opponent to switch his line of attack and score with a lead uppercut to the midsection.

 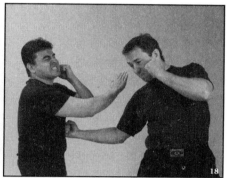

Photo Series 19–20: This example illustrates how, by parrying the opponent's lead hand attack too hard, you knock his arm into your own lead-hand counter.

Photo Series 21: In this example of under-parrying, by failing to parry sufficiently, the opponent's attack still lands.

Parry without any unnecessary tension. Too much force or unnecessary tension in the body will delay your reflexes and reduce your speed.

There are several ways that you can make your parrying more efficient. One way is by including body positioning, such as a slight lean with your parry. Another is by combining some form of footwork, such as sidestepping with your parry.

Photo Series 22–23: This example illustrates how you can support a rear-hand cross-parry by leaning your body slightly to the left.

Photo Series 24: This example illustrates how you can combine your rear-hand cross-parry with a small left sidestep.

The Four Corners

Any fighting style or method that parries and attacks simultaneously will be structurally faster than a style that incorporates a "block first and then attack" structure. Compare the following two photograph sequences. Which is more efficient and economical in terms of structure and movement?

Photo Series 25–27: This sequence illustrates the typical block first-and then hit method used by many traditional martial art systems.

Photo Series 28–29: This sequence illustrates the use of simultaneous defense and attack.

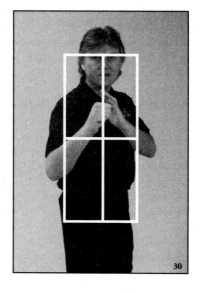

While the "four corners" simultaneous defense and attack structure has its origins in the art of Wing Chun, Lee adapted and modified its usage to fit his requirements in JKD. The four corners structure is based on an imaginary window-frame type structure in front of your body that divides the body into four sectors, commonly referred to as "gates." The body is divided vertically into left and right halves by the centerline (an imaginary line running down the center of your body dividing it into two halves), and marked at the top by a line across the eyebrows, and at the bottom by a line across the groin. Two vertical lines down both shoulders form the outer barriers. A horizontal line midway between the eyebrows and the groin divides the high and low gates. The area inside this frame is your "personal airspace," the area that you need to defend. Anything outside the frame can be classified as "international airspace." **(Photo 30).**

In a right lead, the left upper gate is covered by using a palm-up high *parry (tan sao)* or an outer forearm cover *(biu sao)* **Photo 31**. The right upper gate is covered by using a high cross parry *(woang pak)* **Photo 32**. The lower right gate is covered by a low slapping parry *(ouy ha pak)* **Photo 33**.

The left lower gate is covered by either a low slapping parry *(ouy ha pak)* or a sweeping semi-circular parry which closes the area *(loy ha pak)* **Photos 34, 35.**

Photo 36: Defending Inside High. You can use a high rear-hand palm up cover against a looping swing punch.

Photo 37: Defending Outside High. You can use a high rear-hand cross parry against a lead straight punch.

Photo 38: Defending Outside Low. You can use a low rear-hand slapping parry against a low lead punch to the right side of the body.

Photo 39: Defending Inside Low. You can use a low rear-hand slapping parry against a low lead punch to the left side of the body.

Photo 40: Defending Inside Low. You can use a low rear-hand semi-circular parry against a lead shovel hook to the body.

JKD tends to favor rear hand parries, allowing you to hit simultaneously with the lead hand, as it is closer to the opponent. However, this should not be looked at as an inviolable "rule." At times the lead hand can also be used to parry attacks into the four gates. (**Photo Series 41–44**)

Notice the economy of motion and how little the elbow moves when the four corner parries are being used. This relates to the so-called "immovable elbow" in Wing Chun. Theoretically, the elbow works like a hurricane. The eye of the hurricane (the elbow) is still, but its periphery (the forearm and hand) is constantly moving and exerting tremendous force. The hand and the forearm can move in any direction, but the elbow remains in a fixed position. Any excessive motion opens you up and exposes you to attack (especially if the opponent disengages).

The following series of photographs illustrate the <u>incorrect</u> way to use the four corners.

Photo Series 45–48: Incorrect use of the Four Corners. The wide arm movements are not only uneconomical, but they also expose you to other attacks.

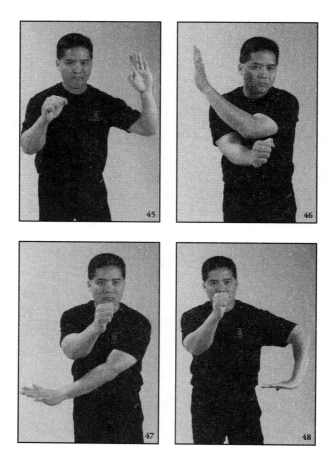

The four corner intercepting hit with parry can be applied three ways (also see section on Counter-Attack):

• Parry followed by intercepting hit.

• Parry and intercepting hit applied together.

• Intercepting hit followed by parry.

Finally, the four corner parries are designed for use against straight thrusts and common street blows. They are not designed for use against tight, compact motions such as a Western boxer's short-range hook punch. If you try to use them against such attacks you may very well find yourself in big trouble.

Photo Series 49–50: If you attempt to use a high palm-up cover against a tight boxing-style hook punch, the blow may go around your arm and still land.

The "Beat" and "Grabbing" Parry

While it was stated at the beginning of this section that parries are light, easy movements, there are two additional types of parries that can also be used. The first is known as a "beat" parry. When using this type of parry you strike the opponent's attacking arm or leg briskly, in order to either knock it aside and secure an opening into which your counter-attack can travel, or draw a particular reaction that you can use to your advantage. The "grabbing" parry can be used to immobilize and control the opponent's arm or leg and allow you to shift into trapping or grappling.

Photo Series 51–53: "Beat" parry. As the opponent punches, you can use a "beat" parry against his attacking arm in order to knock it out of line.

Photo Series 54–55: Grabbing parry. As the opponent punches, you can maintain contact with his arm as you parry it, thereby controlling it.

Distance in Parrying

Any time you execute a parry, you should change the distance in one direction or another. This presents the opponent with a new situation in the midst of his attack, and has a disruptive influence on the penetration, speed, and confidence of the attack. A parry may be combined with a retreat for increased security or with an advance to break into the opponent's attack. Parrying with an advance is more risky because it requires correct judgment of the kind of attack to be expected and of the right moment to parry with the advance. Conversely, moving in with a parry is much more effective for immediate countering, and more surprising to the opponent. Another factor regarding parrying is that if the opponent you are fighting has superior skills or a reach advantage over you, it may be necessary for you to combine the parry with a backward step.

Photo Series 56-58: You can combine your rear-hand cross parry with a small step backward in order to open the distance slightly.

Remember though, if you combine a parry with a retreat, the length of your backward step has to be adjusted to the length of the opponent's attacking movement to ensure that proper distance is maintained for a successful counter-attack. It should

be so short that it not only helps the parry but also keeps you within distance of the opponent, enabling you to reach him with a fast return. If your step is too long, you may put yourself out of range for a fast counter-attack.

In combat, parries should only be used against real attacks. Feints and false attacks can be followed with half-positions. The following training exercise can help you develop your ability to know when to parry:

Face your partner in a ready stance. As your partner slowly strikes to different targets, follow his movements with a parry, but stop when he stops, parrying only the real attacks. Next, have your partner make the same strikes, but don't follow his motion with your parry. Parry only when a real strike comes. This exercise will help teach you to parry at the last moment.

As a final note in parrying, it's important to remember that it can be detrimental to always react to an attack with the same type of parry every time. If you do so, a good opponent will use it against you. So make it a tactical point to mix and vary the types of parries you use, as well as combining them with other defensive methods so that the opponent is always guessing and unable to set up an attacking plan.

Training Tips

- Practice your parries in the following ways: stationary in a ready position; with a retreat; with an advance; after recovering.

- Parry as late as possible, just before the attack is going to land.

- Make economical movements. Avoid over-parrying but make sure your parry is sufficient to deflect the attack.

- Avoid unnecessary tension.

- Support your parries with body angulation and/or footwork.

- Regulate distance when parrying.

- Mix and vary your parries—front hand, rear hand, use of "grab" and "beat" parries, etc. to keep the opponent guessing.

Evasion

According to Academy Award winning screenwriter Stirling Silliphant, who was one of Bruce Lee's private students, "Bruce was a great believer in <u>not</u> being hit. He felt there was no reason ever to be hit unless you failed yourself."

Advocates of blocking may argue that a fighter who is always getting away is certainly wasting or neglecting opportunities to counter, since there's no better moment for a punch or kick than just after an opponent's blow has failed to land. They'll also argue that a fighter who is always getting away very often puts himself out of range, and that since he must come back within hitting distance if he wants to score, he will necessarily open himself up to being hit.

However, it is not necessary to dance back away in order to avoid a punch or kick. The martial artist who practices the art of evasion can escape being hit, and yet stay well within range to counter-attack his opponent. By evading an attack, we mean avoiding it by shifting our body and angling, while remaining within range to counter-attack. The objective is to make the opponent miss with his attack. Why waste your strength and energy and run risks in an attempt to block a blow that you can evade? You may fail to block the attack and may actually stop it with your face or your body, and that is neither profitable nor pleasant. It's also more annoying to an opponent and exhausts him more to miss altogether than it does to have his blows warded off. Following are the basic methods of evasion used in JKD:

The Snap-Away

When using the snap-away, you literally "snap" your upper body backward and away from either a straight or a curved line attack aimed at your head, causing the attack to miss. The rear guarding hand is held in front of the chin for additional protection, but should not reach out to meet the blow. The idea is to not let the force of the punch have any effect on you. Sometimes the snap-away can also be combined with a small step backward.

Photo Series 59–61: You can use an upper body snap away combined with a push shuffle retreat to evade an opponent's lead punch, then use a push shuffle advance to close the distance as you snap in and score with your own punch.

Photo Series 62–64: You can use an upper body snap away to open the distance and cause an opponent's lead straight punch to miss, then snap back in and score with your own lead straight punch.

Photo Series 65–66: The proper distance the rear hand should be from your chin when using it as additional protection during the snap away.

Ducking

Ducking can be used to escape underneath swinging or hooking blows aimed at your head. Ducking is done by bending your waist and shifting your trunk slightly forward, while at the same time keeping your hands high and watching your opponent as the blow continues over your head. A good way to visualize the motion is to imagine that you have a piece of chalk or a pencil sticking out of your forehead, and then simply draw a vertical line down and up with it as you bend your legs. Ducking straight down allows you to counter with either hand, or even shift into grappling. An important thing to remember when ducking under any blow is that you need to be very aware of the possibility that the opponent might fire a knee at your head while you're ducking. So keep yourself well covered with your arms close to your body and be ready to defend if necessary.

Photo Series 67–69: You can duck under an opponent's rear hook aimed at your head and counter with a rear straight punch to his groin.

Photo Series 70–71: Ducking against an opponent's lead and rear high hook punches.

Photo Series 72–74: If you duck under an opponent's punch, be careful in case he suddenly fires a knee upward into your face.

Photo Series 75–77: Another danger in ducking is that an opponent may suddenly slam a downward forearm smash into your neck.

Slipping

Slipping is primarily used against straight shots aimed at your head. Slipping calls for exact timing and good judgment, because to be really effective it must be done so that the opponent's blow barely misses you. However, when used correctly it will surprise an opponent and leave him vulnerable to immediate counter-attack. You can slip to the inside or the outside of an opponent, but the outside is generally safer because it takes you away from the opponent's other arm and leg. You can counter-hit at the same time that you slip, or slip first and then counter-hit. Let's break down how to slip a punch and then look at various ways slipping can be used.

To slip a punch over your right shoulder, drop your weight slightly back onto your rear leg by quickly turning your lead shoulder and body to the left. Your lead foot remains stationary, but your right toe pivots inward. This will cause the opponent's punch to slip harmlessly over your right shoulder.

Photo Series 78–79: How you slip a punch over your right shoulder.

Photo Series 80–81: When the opponent fires a lead straight punch at your head, slip to the outside position, allowing the punch to go over your right shoulder.

To slip a punch over your left shoulder, shift your weight over your lead leg, move your body slightly to the right and forward, and bring your rear shoulder quickly forward. Your rear hip rotates inward, and the rear knee bends slightly to allow the opponent's punch to slip over your left shoulder.

Photo Series 82–83: How you slip a punch over your left shoulder.

Photo Series 84–85: When the opponent fires a lead straight punch at your head, slip to the inside position and allow the punch to slip over your left shoulder.

As opposed to parrying, in which one hand is used in a defensive manner, slipping leaves both hands free to counter with. Sometimes you might slip and counter-attack simultaneously, and at other times you may slip first and then hit.

Photo Series 86–87: Simultaneous slip and hit. When the opponent fires a lead straight punch, you can slip to the outside position and fire your own low lead straight punch into the midsection.

Photo Series 88–89: Simultaneous slip-and-hit. When an opponent fires a lead straight punch, you can slip to the inside position and counter with a low rear cross to the ribs at the same time.

Photo Series 90–91: Slip first and then hit. In this example, when the opponent fires a lead straight punch at your head, you slip to the inside position first, and then counter with a lead shovel hook to the solar plexus.

Sometimes, for added safety, you can combine a small sidestep to the right or left when you slip a punch.

Photo Series 92–93: You can combine a small sidestep to the right as you slip a punch over your left shoulder.

Photo Series 94–95: You can combine a small sidestep to the left as you slip a punch over your right shoulder.

Photo Series 96–97: As the opponent fires a lead straight punch at your head, slip it over your right shoulder while at the same time taking a small left step with your rear foot and firing your lead straight punch to the opponent's midsection.

Finally, when slipping, make sure to keep yourself well covered by holding your hands high to offset any possible counter from the opponent.

Photo Series 98–99: Slipping correctly. By keeping your guarding hand up when you slip, you will be in good position to protect yourself if the opponent suddenly fires a rear elbow smash at your face.

Photo Series 100–102: Slipping incorrectly. If you slip to an inside position against an opponent and either drop your guarding hand or carry your hands too low, you may get hit by an opponent's rear elbow smash to the face.

Bob-and-Weave

As with ducking, the primary purpose of the bob-and-weave is to slide under an opponent's curved line attack and move into close range. The bob takes your upper body forward and inside the circumference of the attacking blow, causing it to miss and allowing it continue over your head without stopping. The weave moves you in the opposite direction of the attacking blow's force. Let's break down the bob-and-weave and look at it in detail.

From your ready position, bob forward and downward by bending your upper torso forward while at the same time bending your legs. Keep your eyes on your opponent and carry your hands high, maintaining a well-covered position, ready to slip at any time if necessary. At the bottom of the bob, weave your upper body either to the right or left—depending upon which direction you want to go—and which direction the blow is coming from. A good way to visualize the bob and weave is to imagine yourself looking at a large clock face, with your head being at 12 o'clock. Bob straight down to six o'clock, then weave to either three o'clock or nine o'clock.

Photo Series 103–106: Illustrates the bob and weave shifting to the left.

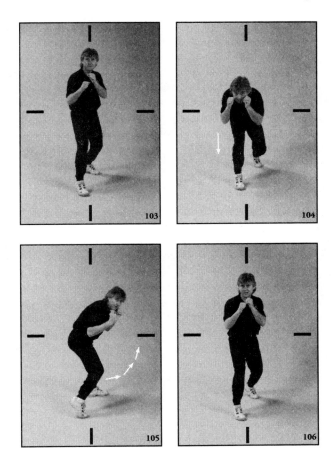

Photo Series 107–110: As a lead hook comes toward the left side of your face, bob forward and weave left, moving underneath and away from the blow. Notice how the forward motion of the bob takes you inside the circumference of the opponent's punch.

Photo Series 111–114: Bob-and-weave with follow-up counter. As the opponent fires a lead hook at the left side of your head, use a bob and weave to evade the blow, then counter with an immediate straight rear cross to the face.

Photo Series 115–118: Illustrates the bob and weave shifting to the right.

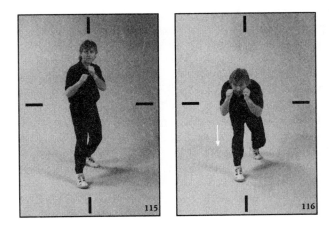

Photo Series 119–122: Against a rear hook coming toward the right side of your face, bob forward and weave right, again moving underneath and away from the blow.

Photo Series 123–126: As an opponent in an unmatched lead fires a lead hook at the right side of your head, use a bob and weave to evade the blow, then counter with an immediate lead hook.

Sometimes, in order to help you achieve a better position from which to counter, a small sidestep can be combined with your weave.

Photo Series 127–129: Illustrates combining a left sidestep with a left bob and weave.

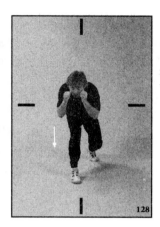

Photo Series 130–133: Against a lead hook to the head, combine a left sidestep with your bob and weave, then counter with a rear shovel hook to the opponent's kidney.

Photo Series 134–136: Illustrates combining a right sidestep with the bob and weave right.

Photo Series 137–140: Against an opponent in an unmatched lead who fires a lead hook at your head, combine a right sidestep with your bob and weave to evade the attack, then counter with a lead shovel hook to the opponent's kidney.

Besides being used with the bob, the weave can also be combined with slipping. For example, you might slip outside the opponent's lead straight punch aimed at your head, then weave under his rear cross to change your position. You can also hit the opponent as you are weaving underneath his attack.

Photo Series 141–144: Hitting on the weave. After using the bob to move inside and under the opponent's lead hook, fire a lead hook to the opponent's stomach as you weave to the outside position. Finish with a rear shovel hook to the opponent's kidney.

Photo Series 145–146: As with slipping, make sure you maintain good defensive coverage when using the bob-and-weave. Don't leave yourself vulnerable to counter-attacks such as a knee to the face.

Training Tips

- Avoid overdoing the evasion business. Do not waste time and do not waste effort.

- Don't make any commitment to an oncoming attack until the last possible moment.

- Make use of your legs when ducking, slipping, and bobbing-and-weaving.

- When slipping a punch try to remain as close as possible to the opponent's attacking arm.

- Maintain good, tight defensive coverage when using any type of evasive tactics.

- Combine counter-hitting with your evasive tactics whenever possible.

- Endeavor never to lose sight of the opponent when evading their attacking motions.

Blocking

The final defensive skill is blocking. When you block an attack you halt it by placing something in its path such as your arm or leg. In Jeet Kune Do, blocking is considered the least efficient of all of the defensive actions, and should only be used as a last resort or if absolutely necessary. Blocking uses force against force and can cause contusions to muscles and bones. If an opponent's blow is delivered with sufficient force, even if you block the blow it will disturb your balance and make countering more difficult. When fighting, the idea is not to wage a war of attrition or see how much punishment you can absorb from the opponent. In terms of combat, it is much better to "give" than to "receive."

Photo Series 147–148: Blocking with the leg. You can lift your lead leg and use your shin to block a rear hook kick aimed at your thigh.

Photo Series 149–150: Blocking with the arm. You can use a lead forearm block against an opponent's rear cross to your body

Training Defensive Skills

In training your defensive skills, the primary objective is to replace instinctive and less effective defensive moves with well-reasoned, effective ones. Your defensive game should be developed by intensive, repetitive practice in order to develop faultless execution of each possible move in all of the categories (e.g., parrying, evading), as well as proper distance and good timing. The development of good defensive methods involves the mechanical aspects of the different parries and evasions, followed by the development of your defensive reflexes. To master the mechanical aspects, repetition of the various defensive actions is required. This should be performed slowly and easily at the beginning with the emphasis on correct hand or body position, and then faster in response to progressively rapid oncoming attacks. To develop good defensive reflexes, you should learn to parry, slip, duck, etc, at the last possible moment, when the attack is only a few inches away, instead of at the very beginning of the attack.

In training, practice with a cooperative partner at first, using varying tempos and rhythm with the various defensive moves. As you get better, work on developing your defensive reflexes by having your partner execute some surprise attacks against you such as attacking into a line other than the designated one. This will help you sense the parry.

Conclusion

It's a known fact that a football team cannot win a game by using pure defense. The same rule applies in fighting. If you only use defense and an opponent throws enough shots at you, no matter how good your defensive skills may be, sooner or later some of his attacks are going to get through and land. A strong attack is always the best and surest defense, for the simple reason that if an opponent's time and attention are fully occupied in protecting himself he will have very little chance of carrying out offensive operations on his own account. So make your defense aggressive in order to frustrate the opponent and disrupt his plans or actions. Even in the midst of defending, constantly look for openings in which to counter-hit. Think of your defense in terms of efficiency. Ask yourself, "What can I get the most out of that requires the least effort?"

Finally, it's important to differentiate between a defensive motion that might be suitable for the ring, and its possible weaknesses for use on the street. For example, a forearm block against a rear cross to the body might be okay if the person you're fighting is wearing nice padded boxing gloves. But against a bare fist or the toe of a hard shoe, the results might not be lees than desirable.

Chapter 4

THE ART OF DISTANCE

"It is essential that each man learns his own attacking and defense distances."
—*Bruce Lee*

There's an old fencing axiom that states, "Whoever controls the distance, controls the fight. And whoever controls the fight, will win the fight." Let's say that I have a sword and my opponent has a knife. If I am able to keep the opponent at long range, the distance for which my weapon is best suited, the odds are that I will emerge the victor in the encounter. If, on the other hand, the opponent can close the distance and get inside to the range that best suits his weapon, then he will probably win.

Consider a confrontation between a boxer and a wrestler. If the boxer is able to keep the wrestler at a range that prevents him from using his grappling skills, the boxer will have the advantage. If, however, the wrestler manages to close the distance and force the boxer into a grappling situation, then the advantage will fall to the wrestler.

In fighting, distance can be defined as the spatial relationship that exists between you and your opponent. This spatial relationship is continually shifting and changing as each of you tries to outsmart the other and either (a) find the correct distance to launch an attack, (b) cause the opponent's attack to miss, or (c) disturb the opponent's plan of action.

Rarely will any of your attacks succeed unless you can position yourself at the correct or appropriate distance. And in order to do that, you need to be able to control the distance. Controlling the distance offers you the ability to pursue an opponent without giving him the opportunity to develop his own attack or to withdraw out of reach of an attack in a split-second. In any combative situation, it's important that you're able to judge the exact distance you are from your opponent at all times.

Distances Defined

At any given moment, the spatial relationship between you and an opponent will fall into one of three distances or ranges: (1) long-range, (2) intermediate or medium-range, (3) close-range.

Photo Series 1–3: Illustrates the three ranges: (a) Long-range (b) Intermediate or Medium range (c) Close-range.

Many people will use terms such as punching-range, kicking-range, trapping-range, grappling-range, and so on when talking about distance. But in reality these are particular aspects of fighting, not distances. For example, I might catch an opponent's leg and apply an anklelock as he attempts to hook kick me in the stomach. In this situation, while the opponent is attacking with a long-range technique, I counter with a close-range technique. Likewise, certain kicks and punches can be used in either long, medium, or close ranges.

Distance will influence not only your movements but also your tactics. Which weapon you choose to use at any given moment is to a large degree dependent upon what range you are in. For instance, you wouldn't want to try to throw a close-range technique such as an elbow to the opponent's head while you are out in kicking range. Likewise, it would be foolish to attempt a long-range kick once the opponent has closed the distance and is about to grab hold of you.

In relation to any opponent you are fighting, at any given moment you will be either "in distance" or "out of distance." "In distance" means that you are within range to reach an opponent, and consequently also within his reach. Unless you are overwhelmingly superior to an opponent or totally outclass him, the only reason you should be "in distance" at any time is because you are either attacking him, or countering his attack. Then you should be gone. Don't stay there. It doesn't matter how fast you can parry, if an opponent is close enough to you and moves first, he will arrive with his attack. For this reason you should always try to prevent the opponent from attacking within distance.

"Out of distance," on the other hand, means that you remain outside of the opponent's effective range, thereby eliminating the threat of being hit. It also means that you will not be in position to hit the opponent until the gap has been somehow bridged. When first facing any opponent, it's always better to be a little too far away than to be a little too close.

The Fighting Measure

In Jeet Kune Do, the distance you maintain against an opponent is referred to as the "fighting measure." This measure, or distance, is governed by several factors. The first is the maximum reach that can be attained with your own weapons. To help you find this, do the following exercise with a friend or training partner:

Stand still and lift your leg, extending it as far outward as you can in kicking position. Pivot slowly in a complete circle and have your friend or partner draw a circle on the ground around you at the length of your extended leg. The circle on the ground indicates the maximum reach of your longest weapon. All of the time an opponent remains outside of that circle he is outside the range of your weapons. However, the moment the opponent moves into your circle, you have two options. You can either (a) fire your weapon, or (b) readjust your distance with footwork.

Photo Series 4–5: The length of your longest weapon, your lead side kick.

Photo Series 6–7: Firing the weapon. When an opponent steps forward into your distance, you fire your lead side kick to the closest target—his lead knee.

Photo Series 8–10: Readjusting the distance. In this case, when the opponent steps into your distance, you use a step-slide retreat to reestablish the distance.

The second factor is the reach of the opponent's weapons. You have to relate to the size of an opponent and the length of his weapons. If an opponent is six inches taller than you and has a reach advantage of several inches, you might be out of distance with regard to your own attacks, but in distance for the opponent's attacks against you.

The third factor concerns the amount of target you have to defend. In boxing, for example, no kicking attacks are permitted, and only certain sections of the torso and head are considered legitimate targets. Therefore, a boxer only needs to be concerned with an opponent's punching attacks to his head and body. In kickboxing, however, the fighting measure has to be expanded due to the fact that kicking and low-line attacks are involved.

Jeet Kune Do deals with combat. It is not about sport. You aren't limited to the confines of a ring. Nor are you concerned with scoring points in a particular fashion, wearing certain safety equipment, or following certain rules and regulations. In JKD, the entire body, from the tip of your head to your toes, is considered a target. The fourth factor is the relative speed and agility of both you and your opponent. If you are much faster and stronger than your opponent, you may shorten the distance. On the other hand, if an opponent is faster than you and has superior skills, you may have to increase the distance.

In JKD, the primary distance that you seek to maintain against an opponent is such that he cannot score a hit on you without first either taking a step forward or making some sort of preparatory move. This is what we refer to as the "brim of fire" line. Of course, maintaining such a distance also means that you cannot hit the opponent without either closing the distance yourself, or luring the opponent into coming forward into range.

Photo Series 11–12: Correct distance. These photos illustrate maintaining the proper distance whereby an opponent cannot reach you with either (a) his lead leg, or (b) his lead hand without first closing the distance.

Photo Series 13–15: Incorrect distance. By remaining too close to the opponent you are in distance to be hit with (a) his lead leg or, (b) his lead hand without him having to close the distance first.

The ability to use distance to your best advantage requires three things:

- Excellent footwork and mobility skills. You need smooth, fast footwork and good balance in order to be able to advance and retreat in and out of distance with respect to both your own and your opponent's reach.

- A precise evaluation of your own distances of attack and defense. You need to know the length of your own weapons.

- A precise evaluation of the opponent's distance of attack. You need to be able to gauge the length of the opponent's attacking weapons.

Distance as Attack

Bruce Lee's study of distance was heavily influenced by Western fencing, which in turn was based upon actually dueling or fighting with swords. By developing lightning fast closing speed, Lee could operate from outside his opponent's reach and stay at a safe distance. According to many of the people who personally trained with Bruce, he could close on a person from a distance of seven to 10 feet away before they could even react. The covering of distance between you and an opponent is known as "bridging the gap."

In bridging the gap, both good timing and proper rhythm are critical. You have to not only choose the perfect moment to attack, but also adjust your rhythm accordingly in order to penetrate the opponent's defenses. There is no time for wasted movement, either. Success in bridging the gap depends heavily on an unnoticeable, smooth start, and perfect harmony of your hand or foot movements. Make sure to "cover" the closing of distance by momentarily distracting the opponent with some kind of motion or action such as a low kick feint or a lead hand feint.

Photo Series 16–17: As you bridge the gap and close the distance against an opponent, use a lead finger jab feint to distract the opponent's attention.

There are several important principles concerning the use of distance as attack. The first principle is that for fastest contact with an opponent, use the longest weapon to attack the opponent's nearest target. Distance is based on the maximum reach you can attain with your longest weapons. In kicking, this could be using the lead-leg shin/knee kick. In striking, it would be using a lead-hand finger jab to the opponent's eyes.

Photo Series 18–19: Illustrates using your longest leg weapon, your lead side kick, to attack the opponent's closest target, his lead knee.

Photo Series 20–21: Illustrates using your longest hand weapon, your lead-hand finger jab, to attack the opponent's eyes.

The second principle is that your attack should be aimed at the distance the opponent will be at when they realize they're being attacked, not the distance prior to the attack. For example, if you aim an attack so that your weapon reaches full extension at the point where the opponent is prior to the attack, all he has to do is shift back slightly and your attack will fall short. However, if you aim your attack several inches behind where the opponent is, even if he shifts back the attack will still land.

Photo Series 22–23: Incorrect gauge of distance in kicking. By aiming your side kick so that it reaches full extension at the distance the opponent's leg is currently located, if the opponent takes a step back your kick will fall short of the target and miss.

Photo Series 24–26: By aiming your kick slightly behind where the opponent is in a ready position, if the opponent takes a step back your attack still lands.

Photo Series 27–28: Incorrect distance in punching. If you aim your punch so that it reaches full extension where the opponent's face is currently located, if the opponent leans back slightly your punch will fall short.

Photo Series 29–30: By aiming your punch several inches behind where the opponent's face is, if the opponent leans back your punch still lands on target.

The third principle is that, when using distance as attack, it's very important to ascertain the opponent's possible reactions to any attacks through the use of feints and false attacks, so as to evaluate the correct attacking distance. For example, does the opponent combine a retreat step with his parry or remain in the same place? Does he try to crash forward into your attack?

Distance as Defense

When using distance as defense, the idea is to frustrate an opponent's attack by either (a) opening the distance using footwork, or (b) closing the distance and smothering an attack before it has a chance to develop. Opening the distance allows you to recognize and analyze the opponent's intentions, speed, reach, etc. Closing the distance allows for immediate counter-attack. Both require sharp awareness and good judgment of the opponent's length of penetration, along with coordinated footwork and good timing.

Breaking the Distance

Once you understand how to control the distance, you can then "break" the distance. There are several ways to do this. The first is by adjusting your footwork. For example, by progressively shortening your retreating steps, an opponent can be brought into range without his knowledge. Or while advancing you may, with a very subtle motion, slide your rear foot several inches further forward. Then as you step again the opponent suddenly finds that you have some-how closed the distance. This is known as "stealing a step."

Photo Series 31–34: By taking progressively smaller steps as you retreat against an opponent, you can cause him to close the distance unknowingly, and bring him into range for your lead straight punch.

Photo Series 35–38: While advancing with a lead straight punch against an opponent who retreats to avoid the blow, subtly slide your rear foot up several inches closer than normal, thereby gaining distance on the opponent without his knowledge. Then step forward with another punch that will land even if the opponent retreats because you have broken the opponent's defensive distance.

A second method of breaking the distance is to create a false sense of distance by firing a weapon that purposefully falls short of hitting the opponent. This can cause the opponent to feel that you cannot reach him, and he may move closer. Creating a false sense of distance can also be an effective strategy, if an opponent is elusive but not aggressive.

Photo Series 39–41: Creating a False Distance. Fire a lead straight punch but keep your shoulder back, giving the opponent the impression that that is as far as your arm can reach. Then suddenly put your full shoulder behind your punch and increase the distance to score.

The third method is to use "broken rhythm" with your footwork. While this is impossible to show in photographs, the process is as follows. First you "lull" the opponent into a controlled rhythm of moving. Then, without any kind of warning, you suddenly break the rhythm at an unexpected moment, thereby gaining a half-cadence advantage on the opponent.

Training Tips

Develop economical, fast footwork and rapid agility.

- Note any continuous or set pattern in the opponent's footwork.

- Train yourself to be aware of the opponent's distance of attack and prevent him from coming into that distance.

- Break the distance by either "stealing a step," creating a false sense of distance, or using "broken rhythm" in your footwork.

- Develop your abilities to "bridge the gap" to their highest level.

Conclusion

Keeping distance plays an important role in fighting, both in attack and defense. The maintenance of the correct fighting distance can have a decisive effect upon the outcome of a situation. The complete fighter must control the distance. Distance perception is the result of complex interrelationships, including keenness of eye, readiness for observation, sense of tempo, rhythm, and space combined with good footwork. It must become instinctive, adaptable, and accurate.

It's essential that you learn your own attacking and defensive distances. Remember, too, that distance varies with each individual and must be evaluated in regards to the individual. In judging distance you have to consider the opponent's speed, his reach, and his ability to cover distance by the length of his forward and backward steps. Finally, you cannot break the distance unless you first know how to control the distance, and the ability to control the distance depends on the way you move and your footwork.

Chapter 5

THE ART OF TIMING

"To move at the right time is the foundation of great skill in fighting…"
—*Bruce Lee*

Would you attack an opponent when he is well prepared, in perfect balance and concentrating on your every move? Unless you totally outclass the opponent, attacking him when he is in such a prepared position could be very detrimental. Instead, what you should seek to do is either catch him physically or mentally unaware, or create a situation in which he is unable to react with a controlled action to your attack. This forces him to move involuntarily and without premeditation. In other words, you must choose the proper time.

Among the factors influencing fighting actions, timing is one of the most important and crucial. It doesn't matter how good your technique is, or how physically fast you may be, if you don't understand timing, or if your sense of timing is poor, all the technique and speed in the world will be of little or no use. An action delivered at the wrong time will not only be ineffective, but may well have disastrous results. To deliver offensive and counter-offensive actions successfully, you need a well-developed sense of timing.

Many people, for example, mistakenly believe that strength and weight are the prime ingredients for hard hitting. While both of these physical attributes are useful, the secret of powerful hitting and kicking lies not in strength or weight, but rather in accurate timing. A blow which knocks an opponent down or even out doesn't need to travel very far. If you land your attack cleanly and crisply and with the full spring of your muscles at the exact moment when the opponent is stepping in towards you or hitting out at you, the impact of your blow will be doubled.

Timing is also the essence of strategy. How often have you watched a more experienced martial artist spar against a less experienced opponent? Many times the more experienced fighter seems able to hit the less experienced opponent at will, sometimes even appearing to move in slow-motion. He seems to outguess the opponent, influencing his reactions and making him do things he doesn't want to do. According to Stirling Silliphant, "Bruce taught me to dissect time into infinite degrees. It's what he called 'playing between the keys' of the piano. It's the understanding that you actually have worlds of time within split seconds to do something else unanticipated while your opponent is committed to his already announced action."

In combat, timing refers to the ability to recognize the most favorable moment and seize an opportunity to attack or counter-attack. This moment may occur naturally in the midst of the fight, such as if the opponent makes some error, loses his focus, or moves too close. Or it may be provoked consciously by an action on your part, such as a feint or false attack. It may be physical (a moment of helplessness) or psychological (a moment of surprise). Either way, in most instances, the favorable moment usually has to be sensed rather than seen.

To fully understand timing you need to recognize that there are actually two types: reaction time and movement time. Both are essential ingredients in developing your sense of timing to its highest potential. Timing and speed are also complementary, so you should cross-reference the training principles covered in this chapter with those pertaining to speed. Let's examine reaction time first.

Reaction Time

Reaction time is the time gap between a stimulus and its response. This stimulus could be visual (such as seeing an opponent's kick coming at you), auditory (such as hearing a would-be attacker moving up on you from behind), or tactile (such as an opponent removing his arm from contact with your own). Total reaction time actually consists of three elements. The first is the time it takes for the stimulus to reach the receivers. This means how long it takes for you to see, hear, or feel the stimulus. The second is the time it takes for your brain to relay the impulses through the proper nerve fibers to the proper muscles. Your brain sends a message to the muscles you intend to use to respond to the stimulus. And the third element is the time taken to get the appropriate muscles into action after receiving the message. So in a combative context, your total reaction time would be from the moment you see, hear, or feel the opponent's action to the beginning of your response.

Improving Your Reaction Time

The time it takes to perceive an attack coming at you usually consumes the greatest part of your total reaction time. So a primary objective in improving reaction time is to increase your speed of perception. There are three main ways of doing this.

The first is to develop your abilities to keep an opponent in your field of vision at all times. In boxing, it's usually the punch a fighter doesn't see that knocks him out. If an opponent is able to maneuver to a position where, for a split-second, you are unable to see him, he may be able to "blindside you" with his attack. So endeavor to never lose sight of your opponent. You must also concentrate on all of the opponent's limbs. If you are too busy concentrating on just his arms you may not see a kick coming. Finally, you should train yourself not to blink as an attack comes towards your face. I learned very early in my own JKD training that the idea of "If I close my eyes he won't see me," doesn't work.

The second way to improve your reaction time is to develop the ability to know beforehand all of the possible movements that a particular weapon may make and the lines it may travel. For example, you should be aware of all the ways that the opponent can kick with his rear leg, and that the leg can travel straight forward, curving from the outside inwards, curving from the inside outwards, upwards, and spinning, and so on.

The final way is to increase your speed of perception and reactive abilities against sudden or unforeseen variations. When you're training, have your partner throw kicks and punches from unusual angles or with off-timing, and train yourself to not be surprised by them.

Constant practice can and will sharply reduce your reaction time. All of the above abilities can and should be developed in the process of perfecting both your technical and tactical actions in training.

Lengthening the Opponent's Reaction Time

An individual's reaction time can become longer under certain conditions. The first is if the person has no training in any type of martial art, and therefore has no idea of what to do or how to do it. The second is if he is tired or fatigued. This could be physical fatigue, mental fatigue, or a combination of both. The third is if the person loses their focus or concentration. And the fourth condition is emotional upheavals, such as if the person loses their cool and gets angry, or if they are afraid.

An opponent's lengthened reaction time can be used to your advantage in timing your attacks or counters because you create a situation in which he is unable to react with a controlled action to your attack. This forces him to move involuntarily and without premeditation. Some moments during which an opponent's reaction time is increased include:

- Immediately after the opponent completes a technique.

- When the opponent is concerned with multiple stimuli.

- As the opponent inhales.

- When the opponent withdraws his energy.

- When the opponent's attention has been diverted, or when he is off-balance physically or mentally.

Movement Time

Movement time is defined as the time it takes to make one simple movement, be it an offensive, countering, or defensive action. Movement time will vary according to the speed of each individual.

Improving Movement Time

As with reaction time, there are several methods by which you can improve and reduce your movement time. The first is by putting yourself in a position, physically and mentally, in which you can attack the opponent in as short a time as that of a reflex action. Avoid having to "set" yourself in order to kick or punch. You shouldn't have to twist or shift yourself into any particular position for the purpose of striking. Instead, you should always be set and in position to put in a punch or kick the moment you see an opening or the opponent makes a mistake. The second is to always be ready, expecting to see an opportunity present itself, and ready to grasp it when it comes.

Lengthening the Opponent's Movement Time

Just as there ways in which you can increase an opponent's reaction time, there are also ways in which you can cause the opponent to lose movement time. These include:

- Jamming the opponent to disturb him and offset his rhythm.

- Using various immobilizations to check his actions and control him.

- Drawing a preliminary reaction, such as a parry in the first half of your attack as seen in the Progressive Indirect Attack.

- Deflecting his movement and scoring with your own.

Photo Series 1–3: As the opponent begins a sidekick, you can slide up and jam his attack then shift into grappling.

Photo Series 4–5: You can use a *pak sao* hand immobilization attack against the opponent's lead arm to check his actions.

Photo Series 6–7: You can use a lead finger jab as a time-hit in order to simultaneously deflect the opponent's attack and score.

Photo Series 8–9: (Use Foot/Hand PIA attack). You can feint a low hook kick to the opponent's groin, and as he attempts to parry, shift your attack to a high lead straight punch to the face.

Timing in Attack and Counter-Attack

There are various times during which your offensive or counter-offensive action may land against an opponent:

Attack on Preparation

An "attack on preparation" is an attack made when the opponent is himself preparing to make an attack. It's an action founded on surprise and performed at the very moment an opponent is concentrating on his attack and before the attack has been fully developed.

A preparation is any movement that a fighter may make to facilitate the development of his offensive action. It might be taking a step forward in an attempt to close the distance to strike, pulling the arm back before punching, or bending the knees before kicking.

To attack on preparation is to attack at the moment the opponent is executing any of these movements. However, it must be done before the opponent launches his own attack. Attacks on preparation necessitate selecting the best moment that the opponent is off balance, is unable to react promptly, and is consequently unable to protect himself. Attacks on preparation should also be kept as simple and direct as possible, as complex attacks might allow the opponent time to reorganize himself. To attack on the preparation requires a total evaluation of the opponent's game so that you can almost anticipate his every move.

Photo Series 10–11: Attack on Preparation. Shoot a lead finger jab to the opponent's eyes as he is stepping forward. (Note that the opponent's own attacking action has not yet been initiated)

Attack on Development

Your action can land when the opponent is in the midst of a movement. In this case the attack has been launched and is already on its way.

Photo Series 12–14: Attack on Development. You can use your lead straight punch counter to score against the opponent as he is midway through his own attack.

Photo Series 15–16: Attack on Development. You can score with a low lead straight punch to the opponent's body as his punching arm reaches full extension.

Attack Upon Completion

Your action can land as the opponent's attack reaches full extension, or even as it begins to withdraw.

Photo Series 17–19: Attack upon completion. In this example, you score with your lead backfist after the opponent completes a side kick, which you avoid by using footwork. (Note: Your counter should land before the opponent's kicking foot touches the ground so that he is still off-balance and less able to defend or counter).

Photo Series 20–21: Attack upon completion. In this example, you score with your own attack after the opponent's punch has missed and he has made the mistake of dropping his arm as it returns.

Photo Series 22–23: Attack upon withdrawal. Many fighters have a tendency of relaxing their guard after completing a technique. In this example, you can score with a low lead kick to the opponent's leg as he is moving backward from a right lead into a left lead.

There are several other favorable moments during which to time your attack. These include when the opponent's attention has been diverted, if he loses his concentration, when he is off-balance, or if he tenses up due to anger or fear.

Photo Series 24–26: Attack when opponent's attention is diverted. In this example, you divert the opponent's attention with a high lead hand feint, then score with a low side kick to the opponent's lead leg.

Photo Series 27–28: Attack when opponent is off-balance. In this example, you time your side kick attack to catch the opponent as he is in the midst of changing his position.

The Unguarded Moment

Good timing depends on registering shifts and lapses in the attention of your opponent, so that you can sense where and how to respond and initiate your own attack.

In his notes, Bruce Lee wrote, "Regard the opponent's concentration as a graph, and avoid the high points and attack in the depressions." Learn to see or sense the opponent's unguarded moment, his "mental gap."

Bob Bremer, one of Lee's Chinatown students, likes to relate that when he was training with Lee, Lee would stand several feet away from Bob and tell him, "I'm going to hit you with a finger jab. When you see me move, block it if you can." Bob would concentrate as hard as he could on seeing the hand move, determined to block it. And every time, no matter how hard he tried, Bruce would hit him. When Bob questioned Lee about it, Lee told him, "I watch you, and for a split-second your mind goes somewhere else and you're not there, and that's when I hit you." So train yourself to keep your attention focused and strike at the moment you sense a fluctuation in the opponent's concentration.

Timing Exercises

Exercises to develop good timing should begin during the early stages of training. The following drills are designed to help you develop your sense of timing. The trainer plays an extremely important role in these exercises by making sure that proper distance is maintained and that the person working the drills develops good form and proper body mechanics. Also remember that repetition without thought can produce an overly mechanical approach.

Exercise 1

In this exercise, your partner uses the focus gloves like "flash cards." The trainer holds both gloves against his chest while his partner moves in front of him in a ready position. The trainer suddenly flashes a target and the partner responds with the correct attack, be it a lead straight punch, side kick, etc.

In a more advanced version of this exercise, the trainer can throw punches or kicks before or after flashing the target so that the partner can work on defense at the same time. This same exercise can also be done using a kicking shield instead of focus gloves.

Exercise 2

In this exercise the trainer presets a focus glove in a particular line, while his partner is moving in a ready position in front of him. The partner attacks the preset line as soon as the trainer takes a step forward. The goal is for the punch or kick to land either slightly before, or just as the trainer's forward motion ends.

Exercise 3

The previous exercise can also be practiced with the trainer taking a backward step instead of advancing. This teaches penetration in attacking the opponent as he is attempting to move away from you.

Exercise 4

In this exercise the partner hits a designated target as the trainer shifts his hand from a high to a low position, or vice versa, or shifts his body in some other way.

Exercise 5

In this exercise the partner practices moving with an opponent and attempts to score as he moves. In this case, cadence and distance must be adjusted to the opponent, and the opponent is not attempting to counter or offset you.

Other timing exercises you can practice include:

Watch TV while moving in a ready position, and hit or kick the second the camera shot changes.

When you are holding equipment for your partner, mentally register the split-second he moves to hit or kick.

Training Tips

- Develop your sensory perceptions (visual, auditory, and tactile).

- Train your eye to observe various things simultaneously.

- Diffuse your attention to see openings or visual cues more quickly.

- Develop the coordination and synchronization of the various parts of your body.

- Train your body to move effortlessly.

- Keep your mind calm so that you can systematize all the thought and stimuli that come into it.

Conclusion

The correct choice of time in moving is a major factor in determining the success of any offensive or counter-offensive action. Your attack or counter-attack must be "on time." That is, neither too late nor too early. Any action, regardless of how technically perfect it might be, can be frustrated or offset by an opponent's parry, block, evasion, or counter if it is timed incorrectly. Therefore, it's essential to time your action at exactly the right moment, when the opponent is unable to avoid being hit. This moment may be physical, such as when the opponent is off-balance or out of position, or psychological, such as if the opponent is surprised or caught unaware. To be able to seize the proper moment, you must maintain a state of constant vigilance and have the ability to control and manipulate distance against your opponent.

By knowing an opponent's timing, you can use a timing that he doesn't expect, thus disrupting his capacities to attack or defend. For example, is he cool and calm, with well-controlled footwork, or nervous and edgy, with a staccato movement pattern? Observe the opponent's movements, then adapt to fit in with his movement and complete your own action.

Timing also requires confidence. You have to have complete faith in your abilities and your tools. How, for example, will you be able to concentrate on tactical actions such as timing if your mind is concerned with whether or not you are able to hit hard enough or fast enough? Choosing the right moment to attack or counter-attack requires trained reflexes and a capacity for lightning-fast judgment and decision, both of which will only come through proper training. A well-trained body and a developed capacity for sudden decision will give you the consistent ability to use timing to your fullest advantage.

Chapter 6

RHYTHM, CADENCE, AND TEMPO

"Every action at the peak of the art of fighting is tempo."
—*Bruce Lee*

An integral part of developing one's timing abilities is the understanding of rhythm, cadence, and tempo. The martial artist who is able to impose his own rhythm on a fight has the advantage of being in control of the situation. To borrow a quote from my close friend, Cass Magda, when explaining the Indonesian martial art of Pencak Silat: "You always want to be the director, never the directee."

In a fight between two combatants, each is attempting to wrest the initiative and dominate the other. In other words: to be the one who directs the situation. Once you have succeeded in directing the opponent, you can suddenly break the rhythm and take him out. Your goal as a martial artist is to reach such a level that you will never be directed by anyone.

The terms rhythm, cadence, and tempo, as used in JKD, are based on their usage in Western fencing, which, in turn, were drawn from Western classical music. While we can define and explain each of them, one cannot show rhythm, cadence, or tempo on paper. It's something that you have to experience and feel. But at least you can get a clear understanding of what each element is, and its relationship in the context of martial arts.

Rhythm

Every action, be it simple or compound, has cadence, articulation, and also its own rhythm. In music, rhythm is the organization of music with respect to time. It's measured movement with uniform recurrence of beat, such as basic "four-four" time, or a "six-eight" beat. Rhythm is composed of beats and rests, or pauses. In life, many of the things we do everyday, we do rhythmically, even if we are unaware of it. We walk rhythmically, we breathe rhythmically, we even talk with a certain rhythmic pattern. And when a martial artist is fighting, they usually do so in some sort of rhythmic fashion.

From a combative aspect, we could look at beats and pauses as action and non-action. The beat would be any action such as a step forward, a punch, a kick, a parry, or even an evasive motion such as a slip or duck. And the pause would be the non-action between one action and the next. The pause is not a lack of action, but an integral part of the overall action. A good martial artist pays as much attention to pause and non-action as to action. Many martial artists make the mistake of attacking continuously without observing the effect, if any, that their attacks are having on the opponent. When you attack, you should always include pauses in the action to allow you to assess the situation, study your opponent's reactions, and adjust if necessary before taking further action.

When sparring, be careful to avoid moving with the same rhythm all of the time. If you do, it will be very easy for an observant opponent to pick up on it and use it to his own advantage. Vary the rhythm of your movements in order to make it as difficult as possible for an opponent to "read" you. Force the opponent to react to you instead of allowing him to dictate his actions.

Cadence

While rhythm is measured movement with uniform recurrence of beat, cadence is the specific rhythm at which a particular succession of movements is executed. A three-punch combination such as a lead jab–rear cross–lead hook, for example, consists of a three cadence—one-two-three. The cadence of any succession of movements or compound attack can be varied by either slowing down or speeding up any of the motions within it. For example, the three-punch combination we mentioned above could be used with the following cadences:

Short—short—short

Long—short—short

Short—long—short

Short—short—long

Short—long—long

Long—short—long

Long—long—short

Long—long—long

Thus, as you can see, in a simple three-motion combination you can have eight different cadences.

Correctly judged cadence permits calm control of every stroke. Ideally, what you want to do in sparring is to impose your cadence on the opponent. This can be done by intentionally varying the cadence of your own movements. It's important to remember, though, that the speed of any particular cadence you use has to be regulated to the opponent you are fighting. If you use a cadence that is too fast you may end up hitting into a still-closed line and in effect, parrying yourself. Whereas if the cadence you use is too slow, the opponent might counter you in the midst of your actions.

It is particularly important to ascertain an opponent's cadence and adapt the rhythm of a compound attack to it. For example, a one-two attack made very fast against an opponent who reacts slowly will often fail, because the attacker returns to the original line to complete his attack before the defender has had time to react at all. The attacker is surprised to find that he is hitting into a closed line which, in fact, has never been opened, because he did not allow time, when making his feint or initial action, for his slower opponent to attempt to parry it. (Cross-reference with timing feints and false attacks) Ideally, the cadence you seek is a speed that is just a little faster than the opponent. In this way you will be ahead of him and he will continually have to try to catch up with you.

Tempo

Tempo represents the most favorable moment in which to initiate an action; namely, that one particular moment when the opponent is either surprised or helpless. At such a moment the opponent is incapable of instantaneous action and his state of unreadiness can be exploited by you. The moment may be physical, or it may be psychological.

Physical unreadiness can be seen. Although the opponent is attentive and observant, he is for some reason either out of balance or in some way delayed, thereby preventing him from executing the desired movement at the proper time. In such a situation he may panic and freeze up or react in a way that is detrimental to himself.

Psychological unreadiness, on the other hand, can't be seen, but only sensed. To sense genuine psychological opportunities is very difficult. Most of the time there are no visible signs, or, at the moment you can see it it's already too late and the opportunity has passed. To be successful in using tempo requires that you are at all times alert and able to coordinate your readiness to act with the opponent's lack of preparedness.

Broken Rhythm

If you and an opponent of equal technical ability are fighting each other, unless one of you is much faster, the confrontation will more than likely result in a stalemate. This is because your offensive and defensive movements work almost in rhythm with that of the opponent. However, if you know how to break the rhythm, speed no longer becomes the principal element in the success of your attack or counter-attack. Broken rhythm can be used to either penetrate an opponent's defenses with your attack, or to offset an opponent's attacking rhythm. It is invaluable in both attack and counter-attack because it enables you to catch an opponent when he is "motor-set," which in turn makes it difficult for him to counter or defend.

There are several ways in which you can break rhythm. After a particular rhythm has been established with regard to any movement or series of movements, it can be broken by either (a) suddenly speeding the cadence of the movement, (b) slowing down the cadence of the movement, or (c) inserting a slight pause or hesitation somewhere in the movement. Let's break down the various ways you can break the rhythm in attack.

To break the rhythm by speeding up the cadence, you first establish a normal rhythm that lulls the opponent into a false sense of preparedness. In other words, he gets used to the speed at which you operate. Then, without warning, you suddenly speed up the movements of your attack and catch the opponent off-guard.

To break the rhythm by slowing down the cadence, you establish a fast rhythm, and then suddenly slow down the movement. Finally, by inserting a hesitation in your movements or making a pause before delivering the final movement you can deceive an opponent as to your intentions. A momentary delay in delivering the final movement may disrupt him and cause him to reopen the line that would have been closed had the rhythm of the attack been constant.

In counter-attack, you can use "hitting on the half-beat" in order to break the opponent's rhythm and disrupt his attack plans. Let's look at the ways we can break the rhythm of an attack comprised of a three-cadence motion; low lead straight punch, high left rear cross, high lead hook. Each motion is represented by one beat:

If you hit the opponent before he completes his first movement, you break the rhythm on the half-beat.

Photo Series 1–2: Breaking on the "1/2 beat." You can use a simultaneous parry and hit to counter the opponent's low lead punch and break the opponent's rhythm on the half-beat.

If you deal with the opponent's first motion, then hit him between his first and second punch, you break the opponent's rhythm on the "one-and-a-half-beat."

Photo Series 3–5: Breaking on the "1½ beat." You can parry the opponent's low lead straight punch, then use a lead finger jab to time-hit him midway through his high rear cross and break the rhythm on the one-and-a-half beat.

If you deal with the first two punches, then hit the opponent between the second and third punches, you break the opponent's rhythm on the "two-and-a-half-beat."

RHYTHM, CADENCE, AND TEMPO

Photo Series 6–9: Breaking on the "2½ beat." You can parry the opponent's low lead punch, cross parry his high rear cross, and score against him with a simultaneous parry and hit midway through his third motion, breaking the rhythm on the two-and-a-half-beat.

Conclusion

A well-developed sense of rhythm, like a well-developed sense of timing, is essential for fighting and should be an integral part of one's combative arsenal. There are numerous training methods that you can use to help develop your sense of rhythm and cadence. One way is to use a metronome that can be adjusted to different speeds, and practice working your motions on the beat and also the half-beat. Another is to make an audio tape of drumbeats or tones using different rhythms and cadences, and work your combinations in time with them. Once you've developed a good sense of rhythm, you can then work on developing your abilities to break the rhythm by using the methods we've just covered.

Appendixes

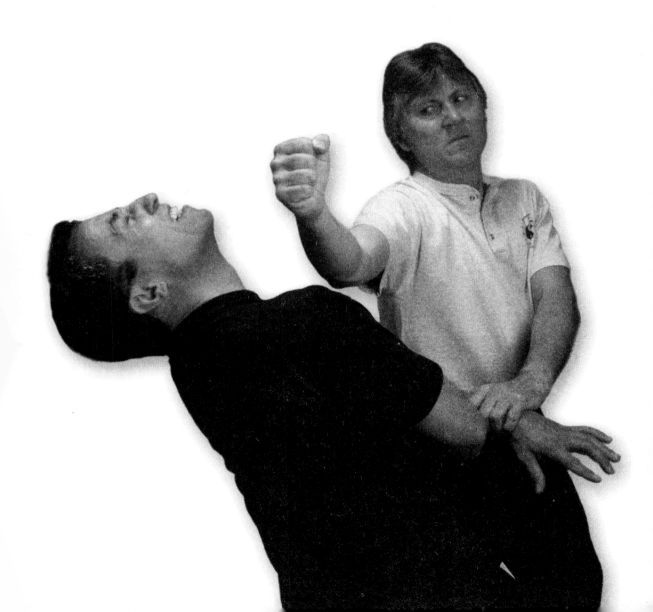

Appendix A

PHILOSOPHICAL TENETS OF JKD

It is through direct understanding and application of Bruce Lee's philosophy that a person becomes liberated from attempting to mimic or imitate Bruce Lee. For this reason I have included in this section explanations of what I consider some of the most relevant philosophical tenets regarding Jeet Kune Do.

"Be Like Water..."

> *"Be shapeless, formless, like water. Now you put water into a cup*
> *it becomes the cup, you put it into a teapot, it becomes the teapot.*
> *Now water can flow or creep or drip or crash. Be water, my friend..."*
> —*Bruce Lee to James Franciscus in "Longstreet" television series*

The water principle served as a base for Lee's study of the martial arts, not only the fluid physical movements of his body, but also in the way he maintained the absolute fluidity of his mind, never sticking, always changing and growing. Why did Lee feel that water was a good representation of the ideals of Jeet Kune Do?

It is at the same time a combination of both *yin* (female, passive) and *yang* (male, active). Nothing is more yielding or softer than water, yet it has the abil-

147

ity to penetrate the hardest rock. Water will find its way through the smallest crack or opening, entering where there appears to be no room. It is so insubstantial that it cannot be grasped. Try to grab a handful of it and it will escape through your fingers without effort. Yet the power of water can inflict great damage. Water is resilient. Kick or punch it and it will yield without hesitation, and then resume itself. Water is an example of wholeness without form, substance without shape. It assumes the form of whatever contains it; a bowl, a cup, a teapot, a valley, etc. The nature of water is to adapt itself instantly to any obstacle in its path. It is thus flexible, adaptable, cooperative, not insisting on its own way.

In the same way that water has no constant form, there are in combat no constant conditions. Fighting is not based on your personal choice or opinions. It changes from moment to moment. Like water, a Jeet Kune Do practitioner should be flexible, adaptable, cooperative and not insisting on his or her own way. Learn how to instantly fill the gaps in an opponent's defense as they are manifested and, like water, adapt to any opponent and flow with every situation that confronts you.

Finally, water, even in a lake, must keep moving. A lake or pond that remains still will stagnate. Running water never grows stale or stagnant. Just like water, we must keep moving on. In your training, you will, at times, experience setbacks, run up against barriers, and become discouraged or frustrated. But you mustn't let these things cause you to become stagnant. You've got to just "keep on flowing."

"Using No Way As Way, Having No Limitation As Limitation."

"Because where there is a 'way,' there lies the limitation, man..."
—Bruce Lee to his student Daniel Lee

Any time a teaching or "way" of doing things is prescribed in inviolable terms or something fixed or "set in stone," the individual's capacity to learn or grow is severely compromised. Even today, many styles of martial arts insist that their way is *the* way, and that there is no other way. Each of these styles claim to possess all of the answers, and their attitude is, "This is the way to do this. This is the best way for all people at all times." Bruce Lee, on the other hand, firmly believed that as each of us is a unique individual with physical, mental, and emotional differences, no single method or "way" of martial arts could contain all the answers or be perfectly suited for every individual.

In JKD, the phrase, "Using no way as way" means to not be locked in or bound to using only one way. It also means not using fixed techniques as your *only* techniques, or blindly copying techniques that may work effectively for another person, but rather continually experimenting and innovating various techniques or body movements to discover your own potential and to find out what works best for you individually. By not attaching yourself to any one style or "way" of doing things, you maintain the freedom to not only use techniques, but also to dispense with them as the moment requires. You find your own way instead of relying on someone else's, and learn to depend upon yourself rather than blindly following anyone else's prescribed approach. As Bruce Lee told his student Daniel Lee, " Man, you know, he is constantly growing. And when he is bound by a set pattern of ideas or "Way" of doing things, that's when he stops growing."

In JKD, the phrase, "Having no limitation as limitation" deals with facing various barriers and obstacles that you will come up against as you pursue the mastery of martial arts. As you travel down the road towards proficiency and mastery in the martial arts, you will undoubtedly find yourself coming up against barriers (both internal and external) that will attempt to limit your growth. These barriers might be physical, such as a lack of flexibility; mental, such as being overly conscious of our actions as we are learning; or emotional, such as overcoming the fear of getting hit while sparring. Most of the time our limitations are self-imposed. We erect our own barriers by saying such things as, "I'm not flexible enough," or "I'll never get it." How you deal with each of the barriers you face will determine whether it becomes a limitation or not. You should look at any current limitation you might have as only a temporary condition, and use it as a building block to help you achieve your true potential.

The Three Stages of Cultivation

Bruce Lee believed that, in the study of martial arts, a person moving toward proficiency passes through three phases, which he termed "the three stages of cultivation."

The first phase or stage is the primitive stage, or the "stage of original ignorance." At this stage the person knows nothing about the art of combat such as proper on-guard positioning, how to punch or kick correctly, or how to parry or evade a blow. When he is attacked he simply blocks and hits instinctively, with no concern for proper form or what is right or wrong. According to Lee, while his actions might not be considered scientific, or for that matter even very functional, his responses are natural and his defenses and attacks are fluid. In other words, he is being himself. At this stage, a punch is just a punch, a kick is just a kick.

The second stage is referred to as "the stage of sophistication" or "the mechanical stage." This stage occurs when a person begins training, and is taught how to stand, different methods of moving, various punches, kicks, strikes, etc. During this stage of training, while the student acquires the scientific knowledge of combat, he loses his original self and sense of freedom, and tends to become very "mechanical," both in thought and actions. He becomes very technique-oriented and his mind is constantly stopping to analyze and calculate. At this stage, a punch is no longer just a punch, a kick is no longer just a kick. It's now a "Wing Chun vertical punch" or a 'Taekwondo side kick." The unfortunate thing is that many students remain in this stage because they feel secure there, and thus never evolve to the next stage.

The third and final stage is called the "stage of artlessness," or the "spontaneous stage." This stage occurs when, after many years of training and practice, the student realizes that what he is doing is nothing special, and that a punch is just a punch, a kick is just a kick. In the third stage the student transcends mechanical technique and becomes formless, like water. In the same way water adjusts and adapts itself to fit any container, the student is now capable of adjusting and adapting to any opponent. At this final stage the student returns to his true self, and regains his original freedom to honestly express himself.

"Learn the Principle. Abide by the Principle. Dissolve the Principle."

The above quote deals with the learning process you go through as a martial artist. In the beginning, you must consciously learn specific techniques or principles. These might include things such as the use of the vertical fist punch, proper body mechanics, good balance, non-telegraphic motion, proper defensive coverage, etc. You "learn the principle" only by *doing*.

To "abide by the principle" means that you practice the technique or principle until you can apply it successfully in all types of situations. It means practicing to develop the understanding of not only the "how," but also the "why" and "when."

"Dissolving the principle" means that you are no longer even aware of it. You've made the technique or principle your own without being bound by it. You're free to use it or not use it as you like. Having assimilated the principle, you begin to improvise, to move away from the techniques with a sense of freedom and imagination.

"Hack Away the Non-Essentials."

Daily decrease is one of the most important principles of Jeet Kune Do. In relating this idea to his students, Bruce would often use the analogy of a sculptor who, in creating his work, does not keep adding clay to his work, but rather carves away at it, bit by bit, until the truth of his creation is revealed without obstructions. In other words, he hacks away the non-essentials.

As with the learning of any art form, a certain amount of accumulation is necessary during the beginning stages. You cannot hack away if you have nothing to begin with. A painter has to learn the various strokes and how to mix different colors. A musician has to learn the various notes, scales, and chords. And as a martial artist, you first have to learn the fundamentals of fighting out of which you can then progress. However, accumulation of knowledge is not synonymous with proficiency. Many martial artists are always adding more and more techniques, forms, etc. In learning, the importance of the quantity of knowledge decreases near the top where the skills already learned are refined and honed to expertise. If you're always adding, you will never have time for refining what you have. Don't allow the additive process to be merely the cultivation of memory.

The operative questions you should ask yourself with regard to your training, are: "How much do I need?" and "Does this make me better?" Your goal is to be fully functional in a real combative situation. Make a clear distinction between what is essential to you and what is not.

The Three Stages of Technique Training

In Jeet Kune Do, technical development is broken down into three stages. The first stage is "Synchronization of Self." The objective at this stage of training is for the student to synchronize or regulate the motion into his being. During this stage the student works on developing correct form, which includes proper body mechanics, precision, and the most efficient manner in which the motion may be used. It is getting the maximum results with a minimum of lost motion and wasted energy. At the same time the student is gradually and progressively increasing his speed.

The second stage is "Synchronization with the Opponent." During this stage the student works on developing his timing, which means the ability to seize an opportunity when it is presented or created. He also works on the maintenance of the correct distance between himself and the opponent.

The third stage is "Application under Fighting Conditions." In this stage the student works on applying the motion under combat-like conditions, with your opponent attempting to provoke errors on your part by blocking, evading or countering with timing and distance.

The Cornerstones of Jeet Kune Do:
Non-Classical, Directness, Simplicity

A cornerstone is an essential foundation stone that marks the beginning of building. In Jeet Kune Do, the cornerstones are Non-Classical, Directness, and Simplicity.

"Non-classical" refers to the principle that in JKD there are no "set," classical postures or exotic stances that a person has to learn to twist into. Everything is natural, mobile, and fluid. Nor are there any classical forms or cooperative, two-man rhythmical sets that are artificial and mechanical. Instead, there is relation-

ship with an "alive," moving opponent and the use of broken rhythm. You are interested in feeling what "is" and not "doing" what was or might be.

"Directness" refers to the principle that in JKD everything is stripped to the essentials. There is little or no passive defense because blocking is considered least efficient. There aren't any fancy or ornate techniques that require move after move. If someone grabs you, you hit him. In other words, do what comes naturally and don't waste time.

"Simplicity" refers to the principle of expressing the utmost with the minimum. Ask yourself, "If something takes three moves, can I simplify it to accomplish the same results with two moves, or even better, one move?" Simplicity also means that instead of continually increasing by accumulating more and more techniques, etc., you minimize by decreasing to the absolute essentials and returning to your original freedom. In Jeet Kune Do, to reduce things to the minimum is the maximum.

Appendix B

MAKING BRUCE LEE'S NOTES WORK FOR YOU

In order to get the most out of JKD it is essential to know how to make Bruce Lee's notes work for you—how to bring them to life and use them to help you achieve your fullest potential as a martial artist. Lee's notes have been likened to guideposts, or clues, that can lead an individual to their own self-expression in the martial arts. But guideposts do a person little or no good if they don't know how to read or interpret them correctly. So the first thing that needs to be understood is how to study Lee's notes. This is not as easy as it sounds. When reading Bruce Lee's notes, three intrinsic principles should guide your study. These principles may, in the beginning, require several separate readings but in time can be done concurrently. The three principles are as follows:

Understand the notes: You need to comprehend thoroughly and perceive clearly the nature of what you're reading. What are the particular writings or notes you are studying saying?

Interpret the notes: The word "interpret" in this case means, "to bring out or explain the meaning of something." In other words, what do the notes you're studying mean? In martial arts it seems that many times people rush to the application stage of Lee's teachings and bypass the theoretical stage. They want to know what the technique means to them before they understand what Lee intended it to mean.

Evaluate the notes: To evaluate something means to judge or determine its worth or quality. In other words, is the given principle right or wrong for them? Is it valid or not? Unfortunately, many people tend to skip over the first two principles and jump right into evaluating Lee's notes. They judge a particular concept to be right or wrong before they understand what it says or before they interpret its meaning.

The above three intrinsic principles are, however, by themselves, inadequate. To study Bruce Lee's notes successfully and get the most out of them, a person also needs three important extrinsic aids. These aids are:

Experience: Experience is the only way to interpret and relate what has been read. A person who has little or no experience in martial arts and/or philosophy is going to be at a distinct disadvantage in understanding, interpreting, and evaluating Lee's notes. I may be able to tell you what I like or don't like about a particular painting by a master like Van Gogh, but I will not be able to interpret and evaluate the painting like a person who has and education and background in fine arts. Experience that has been understood and reflected upon informs and enlightens your study.

Other Books and Writings: Books and writings that precede or advance the subject you're studying can be very significant. Very often books or notes can have greater meaning when they are read in relation to other writings. I have had the privilege of perusing the books in Bruce Lee's personal library at great length. But I have also established my own library that includes books on martial arts, Western fencing, physical fitness, kinesiology, philosophy, and psychology. Studying and analyzing these books has unquestionably helped to increase my understanding of Lee's notes. Bruce Lee always approached a subject wanting to know as much as possible about it and with an open mind ready to absorb new information. If he were alive today, there's no doubt that he would avail himself of the most up-to-date information including books, videos, films, and whatever else was related to whatever subject that interested him or that he was studying. And you should follow his example and do the same thing.

Live discussion: The final extrinsic aid is live discussion, which means the interaction that occurs among individuals as they pursue a particular course of action. My close friends Cass Magda and Del Pollard and I have spent countless hours discussing JKD, sometimes amongst ourselves, and other times with other friends or students. When we discuss and debate certain issues, techniques, or philosophical attitudes relating to JKD, many times new insights emerge that might have never occurred without this type of exchange.

As important as it is to successfully research Lee's notes, however, it is equally important to know how to use them. The first step of this process is to read Lee's notes without trying to fit them into established categories. The goal here is to simply grasp the content of the material, the essence of what is being presented, and to understand it. Expect to hear new things in new ways when you read the notes at different times and don't be concerned if you don't get some things in the first reading. It might take several readings before you fully comprehend something. All of us have had the experience of reading something over and over and then, all of a sudden, understanding what it means. This "Wow, now I get it!" experience of understanding catapults you into onto a new level of growth and freedom. You might find it useful each time you read the notes to use a differently colored pen to mark certain things that stand out to you at that time. Another idea is to keep a journal or notebook handy to jot down thoughts and impressions that occur while reading.

The next step is to investigate why Lee drew a particular essence from an art or why he chose to absorb something into his own art. It's important here to recognize the difference between absorbing and simply adding. Bruce did not add something simply for the sake of adding it. To "absorb" something means, "to take in and incorporate; to assimilate." To "add" means to take in and unite so as to increase the number, size, etc. Ask yourself, "What is it about this particular technique that Bruce Lee felt was useful or valid to what he was doing?" Analyze it by breaking it down into its component parts and examining it to find out its interrelationship with other material in Lee's notes.

The third step is to apply what you are studying. Theory without application means nothing. You've got to take the material you're investigating onto the floor and test it. You need to see if, and how well it works under pressure and in realistic situations. Keep in mind, too, that just because you may not be able to do it or use it at that particular moment, doesn't mean that it's not valid or that it's no good. If your instructor shows you how to do a spinning rear kick and then you try it and miss the target completely, don't immediately respond with, "Oh, that's stupid. It doesn't work."

The final step is evaluation, in which you judge the value of the material for a given purpose. Ask yourself, "Is this particular principle or technique valid or not? How does it relate to me? Does it have application to what I'm doing?" If, for example, the particular style of martial art you practice doesn't believe in the use of hand immobilization attacks, then sensitivity training such as *chi sao* may have no application for you. Keep in mind, though, that just because something might not have an application for you, that doesn't mean it won't have an application for someone else. The following are some pitfalls you should try to avoid when studying and/or using Bruce Lee's notes:

- Simply memorizing and regurgitating Lee's words, ideas, etc. Anybody can repeat someone else's words by rote. Remember, it's not how much fixed knowledge or information you have accumulated, it's what you can use and apply that counts.

- Taking the material in Bruce Lee's notes to be the "Bible" of martial arts. Some people approach JKD very dogmatically and with the fundamentalist view that "If it's not in the *Tao of JKD,* or if it's not in Bruce's writings, then it's not JKD." This is the very antithesis of Lee's teachings. Bruce was a seeker of truth. To him, each thing he wrote down represented *a* truth, not *the* truth. No one has a monopoly on truth. There is no "one way."

- Thinking that Bruce Lee's notes are all there is to his way of martial arts.

- Adding your own interpretation to Bruce Lee's material. I am not saying that you shouldn't interpret Lee's material. I am simply reminding you to keep things in proper context. Many times people read something with an eye towards finding support for what they themselves are doing. For example, in Lee's notes it states, "Investigate into fighting from the ground... develop such mastery that one can fight safely from the ground." But Lee doesn't make a point of telling you to study any particular style of ground-fighting or martial art that includes ground-fighting. The point is to hear what Bruce Lee is saying, not what we want him to say.

- Solidifying Bruce Lee's guideposts into laws. Bruce changed his mind about publishing his notes when he came to the realization that trying to encapsulate fighting into words was like trying to capture something on paper that is alive and constantly changing. It was, he concluded, "like attempting to tie a pound of water into a manageable shape." So don't calcify what should remain alive and growing.

- Starting from a conclusion. Remember, to taste someone else's tea you must first empty your cup of preconceived ideas, notions, etc. Begin with an open mind.

Bruce Lee's notes are like an extension of Bruce himself. They describe the direction of his studies and shed light on his own process of intellectual growth and development as a martial artist. As such, they can serve as a pipeline to his way of thinking, feeling, and researching. Bruce's notes can also act as a navigational guide, like a compass, which can help direct you to where you want to be as a martial artist. If you know how to use a compass, even if the terrain changes, a road becomes blocked, or a detour arises, you can still remain on course toward your ultimate destination. In order to do that, however, you must know where it is that you want to go and whether the goal is physical, mental, emotional, or spiritual. Once you know that, then you can take all of the information in Lee's notes and consider it; debate it, turn it upside down; look at it from your own perspective; refine it to suit you; rearrange it; keep what you think will work for you; and even throw some of it out (just make sure you know why you're throwing it out).

Don't allow anyone to simply hand you the truth. It cannot be done. Take an experiential attitude and find out for yourself what works for you. See Bruce Lee's notes as a literary work in progress, not as something that was finished or completed. Remember, "If you understand it and can use it, it belongs to no one; it's yours."

Appendix C

ESSENTIAL QUALITIES

While physical technique and tactics are the main components of JKD training, there are numerous essential qualities, both mental and physical, that a martial artist should develop in order to actualize their fullest potential. The following are brief descriptions of each of these various qualities.

1. Speed

Movement speed is the ability to generate bodily movements in the shortest possible time. Speed is one of the deciding elements in maximum martial arts performance.

2. Power

Power is the ability to exert your strength quickly. It is also referred to as speed-strength. The primary key to power is to develop the greatest amount of force in the shortest amount of time.

3. Endurance

Endurance is the capacity to resist fatigue. High levels of endurance facilitate the mastery of a lot of hard work during a training session and allow you to maintain high-quality movements for the entire workout. Well-developed endurance abilities are also important for rapid recovery following a hard workout.

4. Coordination

Coordination is the ability that allows you to integrate all the powers and capacities you have into doing something effectively.

5. Precision

Precision is accuracy in movement or projection of force. It means being able to place your weapon of attack exactly on a desired target.

6. Balance

Balance is the quality of achieving an inner relationship between all the points of your body. It is an awareness of where you are in time and space.

7. Body Feel and Good Form

Body feel and good form both relate to the quality of your movements. They mean finding the most efficient manner to accomplish an action with the least amount of lost motion and energy.

8. Flexibility

Flexibility refers to the elasticity of muscles and the range of motion of joints. The more flexible a person is, the more freely he is able to move and the less likely he will be to pull or tear something while training.

Appendix D

AWARENESS TRAINING

"A good fighter must sense rather than perceive the chance to strike."
—Bruce Lee

While the preceding quote concerns the timing of one's attack, an essential prerequisite for achieving a high level of skill in this area is good awareness. Awareness keeps you "in tune" with an opponent, allowing you to be consciously informed of his movements, actions, and reactions. It also keeps you informed about any impending action the opponent might take, and the better informed you are about the opponent's actions or impending actions, the better equipped you are to deal with him. The split-second or momentary edge gained by such increased awareness can make the difference between success and failure of your own actions, and possibly between victory and defeat in a fight.

Awareness training has always been an integral and important part of the JKD curriculum. Exercises to develop or enhance your skill in this area should begin at the very start of your martial art training, and should also be maintained even by advanced martial artists. Bruce Lee himself stated, "As I get older my speed may decrease, but my awareness will increase."

The objective of awareness training is to sharpen your senses of perception such as sight, hearing, and touch, so that you can recognize, identify, and react to an opponent's moves instantaneously without thinking or being bound by what Bruce Lee referred to as "psychical stoppage."

Before we go any further, we need to differentiate between awareness and concentration. Concentration is a narrowing of attention, and it tends to focus on one thing at a time to the exclusion of everything else.

Awareness, on the other hand, is total and excludes nothing. It takes in everything. If you concentrate on an opponent, you focus solely on him, and shut your mind to everything else that might be taking place around the two of you. With awareness, you take in not only your opponent, but everything else as well. This can be extremely useful if you are in a situation in which you are fighting more than one opponent at the same time. In JKD, it is often referred to as "having a loose, pliable awareness." In fact, there are three major types of awareness: visual, auditory, and tactile. Each is important and should be developed to a high level.

In awareness training, some form of cue is used as stimuli to signal an opening against an opponent. The objective is for the student to reduce the time it takes for him to react to the stimuli. The following exercises are designed to help develop or enhance your skills in one of the types of awareness.

Visual Awareness

In combat, you use two types of vision. The first is central vision, in which your eyes are fixed on a central point—be it the opponent's eyes, or somewhere on his body. The second is peripheral vision, in which case, although your eyes are fixed on one point, your attention is expanded over the entire area. While central vision is clear and sharp, peripheral vision is more diffuse. You should train both types of vision.

One way to train your visual awareness with a training partner is to stand about five feet in front of your partner, moving with small motions in a ready position. As soon as your partner makes any kind of movement with his body, such as dropping his arm, turning his head, etc., respond with your action, be it a kick or punch or whatever. As you get better at this your partner can make his motions progressively smaller in order to increase the difficulty of the exercise.

Another way to train visual awareness is to use a flashlight in a darkened room. Keep moving in an ready position while facing a wall upon which your partner is shining the beam of a flashlight, moving it all around. The moment the light stops moving, react with a punch or kick.

You can also work visual awareness training against equipment such as the heavy bag. For example, you can move in front of a heavy bag while your partner holds the bag from behind. The moment he removes one hand from the bag, or lifts one foot, respond with an attack.

To train your peripheral vision, stand facing a wall and concentrate your central vision upon a designated spot, while your partner moves off to your side, until you can just see him with your peripheral vision. You should just be able to see him while keeping your eyes looking straight ahead. Your partner then draws large letters or numbers with his hand, and you try to read the letters or numbers while still looking straight ahead.

If you don't have a training partner, you can use your television set to give you a visual cue. Move in front of it in a ready position, and the moment the shot on the TV changes, respond with your attack. (Although don't watch something like music videos because they usually switch shots every couple of seconds, and you will probably become exhausted in no time.)

Auditory Awareness

Many people fail to realize the importance of auditory awareness. However, it's been proven that people react faster to an auditory cue than to a visual one (hence the switch from using a flag to using a pistol to start a race in athletics.) Some people feel that no need exists to develop auditory awareness. But auditory awareness can be extremely useful if and when you find yourself in a situation in which for some reason your visibility might be restricted (such as being poked in the eye, or having dirt thrown in your eyes), or if you are fighting at night in an unlit room or a dark alleyway.

To train auditory awareness, a sound cue is used as a stimuli to signal an opening against an opponent. If you have a partner, the partner can use either a voice command as the stimulus, or hit clackers or a drum to create a sound that you react to. If you don't have a partner, you can make a tape of a particular sound that you then react to.

Tactile Awareness

Tactile awareness is a heightened sense of touch. You become very sensitive to the movements and energy of the opponent's arms or body motions. This can be very helpful for aspects of fighting such as trapping and grappling. Tactile awareness can be increased by specialized training exercises such as *chi sao,* harmonious spring drill, and other forms of sensitivity training.

In JKD, one of the primary uses of Hand Immobilization Attack or "trapping hands" is to offset or counter what we refer to as "block-and-hit" martial art systems. And in using trapping two of the most important training principles you need to understand and have a good working knowledge of are:

- The Swinging Gate/Hinge Principle.

- The Ball-and-Socket Principle.

Both of these principles are essential for heightened tactile awareness and superior trapping skills. Before we explore these principle in more detail, let's look at how the elbow joint works.

The primary motions of the elbow joint are (1) Flexion, bending the arm and moving the forearm toward the biceps, and (2) Return from flexion, straightening the arm by moving the forearm away from the upper arm. Sometimes return from flexion is also referred to as extension, but in reality the forearm cannot extend without first being flexed. The elbow is also involved in supination and pronation, which involves turning the hand to a palm–up or palm-down position.

The Swinging Gate/Hinge Principle

When a force is exerted inwardly against the outside of your forearm, the elbow acts as a "hinge" on a door or gate, and allows the arm to bend and let the force continue in the direction it is traveling without affecting the rest of your body.

If you want to test this principle, lock your arm out straight like an iron bar and have your friend or training partner exert hard inward pressure against the outside of your forearm. If you keep your arm rigid you will feel the force affect your entire upper body. Then have the person do the same thing again, but this time visualize that your elbow is a hinge and your forearm is a gate. The more pressure the person exerts against your forearm, the faster it should flex and allow the force to continue through without affecting the rest of your body.

The Ball and Socket Principle

When a force is exerted against the inside of your forearm, the elbow cannot bend in the opposite direction toward the triceps. In this case the elbow does not work like a hinge, but rather like a ball-and-socket joint. As with the Swinging Gate/Hinge Principle, the harder or more forceful the pressure exerted against your forearm, the faster it should move, allowing the force to continue through and dissipate.

Training Aid

A good way to practice both the Swinging Gate Principle and the Ball and Socket Principle is to stand facing a partner with one arm extended in a straight punch toward the partner's face. The partner then gives you pressure against either the outside or inside of your forearm, and you respond by using either the Swinging Gate or the Ball and Socket Principle. A more advanced way of practicing the same exercise is to close your eyes so that you cannot tell in advance on which side of your forearm the force is going to be exerted. In this way you no longer see but instead feel the force and respond accordingly.

Both of the above principles are perfect examples of another JKD principle in action. That is the "Bamboo Principle." When force is exerted against bamboo, it neither stubbornly resists the force nor collapses completely before it. Rather, it gives way to the force, allows it to dissipate, and then springs back to its original position.

Two things that can help increase your awareness abilities are:

- Maintaining a loose, relaxed yet ready position at all times.

- Maintaining proper focus of attention.

By "proper focus of attention," I mean having your mind on the task at hand. If your mind is busy thinking about other things such as the argument you had with someone earlier, or the problems you are having with your car, your focus will be split.

Conclusion

All three types of awareness—visual, auditory, and tactile—are essential for a martial artist's overall skills. So you should try to include some form of awareness training in each workout if possible.

Conclusion
WHAT IT ALL AMOUNTS TO...

Jeet Kune Do is about total and complete freedom. The most fundamental principle of Bruce Lee's art is that, as a living and a creative individual, you should not be bound by a prescribed set of rules or techniques, and should be free to explore and expand. Learning and absorbing useable knowledge is not located within the structure of any one style or system. As Lee himself wrote, "Styles are conclusions, but like our life, the truth of martial art is a process."

As a martial artist you owe allegiance not to style, but to truth. And the discovery of truth in martial art, like life itself, is an individual process. You have to discover and experience it by yourself. Nobody can "give" truth to you, be it Bruce Lee, myself, or even your own teacher. You get "it" from yourself. And simply copying Lee's movements, ways, and methods will be of little or no avail in your own process. The goal is to discover through your own experiences, and through what you learn from those experiences, the cause of your own ignorance. Jeet Kune Do is experiential. You have to feel it from within. And each person will feel it differently. You can talk about it and theorize about it forever, but it doesn't mean anything. So awaken yourself to your own personal potential to become totally free (in mind, body, and spirit).

These two volumes, like the videotapes they were written to accompany them, and all other materials pertaining to Jeet Kune Do for that matter, should be considered nothing more than "a finger pointing to the moon." Remember not to gaze too long or too intently at the finger, because in so doing, you will miss all the heavenly splendor.

I wish you well on your journey.

For information concerning class or personal instruction, seminars and workshops, and instructor certification programs, contact Chris Kent at:

Kent Institute of Martial Arts
3015 W. State Street
Boise, ID 83703
(208) 424-0322
e-mail: kentinstitute@rmci.net
website: chriskentjkd.8k.com